# Skills Plus

## Skills Plus

## Listening and Speaking

**Advanced**

David Briggs
Paul Dummett

Heinemann

PHOTOCOPIABLE

Heinemann English Language Teaching

A division of Reed Educational and Professional Publishing Limited

Halley Court, Jordan Hill, Oxford OX2 8EJ

OXFORD MADRID FLORENCE ATHENS PRAGUE SÃO PAULO MEXICO CITY CHICAGO
PORTSMOUTH (NH) TOKYO SINGAPORE KUALA LUMPUR MELBOURNE AUCKLAND
JOHANNESBURG IBADAN GABORONE

ISBN 0 435 25009 4

Text © David Briggs, Paul Dummett 1995

Design and illustration © Heinemann Publishers (Oxford) Ltd 1995

First published 1995

All rights reserved; no part of this publication may be reproduced, stored in a retrieval system, transmitted in any form, or by any means, electronic, mechanical, photocopying, recording, or otherwise, without the prior written permission of the publishers.

**Permission to copy**

The material in this book is copyright. However, the publisher grants permission for copies of pages to be made without fee on those pages marked with the PHOTOCOPIABLE symbol.

Private purchasers may make copies for their own use or for use by classes of which they are in charge; school purchasers may make copies for use within and by the staff and students of the school only. This permission does not extend to additional schools or branches of an institution, who should purchase a separate master copy of the book for their own use.

It is permitted for a school to make a copy of audio material, keeping the original as back-up. Only one copy may exist at any one time. A school may copy different parts of an original audio tape onto several cassettes providing that no part of the original exists in more than one copy at any one time.

For copying in any other circumstances, prior permission in writing must be obtained from Heinemann Publishers (Oxford) Ltd.

Designed by Annette Peppis

Cover design by Stafford & Stafford

Illustrated by: Juliet Breese, Debbie Clark, Caroline Harrison, Alan Rowe, Shirley Walker

**Acknowledgments**

The authors would like to thank Ian Thompson, Vincent Gillespie and the staff of Regent Oxford School of English for their contributions.

The publishers would like to thank the following for permission to reproduce their material:

Jonathan King, Claire Rayner and the BBC for *Myself when young* (Unit 1); Adrian Underhill for the phonetics chart (unit 3); Bill Bryson for the extract from *Neither here nor there* (Unit 5); Bill Oddie, Richard Vaughan and the BBC for *Breakaway* (Unit 6); *Beloved* by Toni Morrison, reproduced by permission of Chatto & Windus Ltd (division of Random House) and International Creative Management Inc. USA, © 1987 Toni Morrison (Unit 7); Edward Blishen, Michael Meyer, Timberlake Wertenbaker and the BBC for *A good read* (Unit 7); Susie Maguire and the BBC for *The way I met Sean Connery* (Unit 15); Stephen Fry, Paul Merton, Nicholas Parsons and the BBC for *Just a minute* (Unit 17); *Private Eye* for the six cartoons by Heath, McLachan, ffolkes and Cliff (Unit 18).

Whilst every effort has been made to trace the owners of copyright material in this book, we should be grateful to hear from anyone who recognises their copyright material and who is unacknowledged. We shall be pleased to make the necessary amendments in future editions of the book.

Printed in Great Britain by Thomson Litho, East Kilbride, Scotland
Bound by Hunter and Foulis, Edinburgh, Scotland

97 98 99 10 9 8 7 6 5 4 3 2

# Contents

Notes to the Teacher

| Unit | Listening type | Language focus | Speaking activity |
|---|---|---|---|
| 1 People:<br>Jonathan King | A radio interview with a pop personality. Listening for an impression of the speaker's personality. Fast delivery (**). | Adjectives and idiomatic phrases describing personality; positive and negative connotations. | Describing someone you know well. |
| 2 People:<br>Personality quiz | Listening to a personality questionnaire on radio. The interviewee speaks with a regional accent (*). | Adjective-noun word building. | Carrying out a questionnaire. ✓ |
| 3 Language learning:<br>English pronunciation | 1 Interview with phonology expert. Listening to a description of the sounds of English. Clear, informed speaker (*).<br><br>2 Nine short extracts featuring different accents (*). | Phonological terms. | 1 Talking about your own language.<br><br>2 Reading a poem aloud. |
| 4 Language Learning:<br>Learning vocabulary | A Lecture. Listening and taking notes. (***). | Explaining and defining. | Word game: Call my bluff |
| 5 Travel:<br>An American's view of Europe | Monologue. Listening to a humorous analysis of European life. American speaker (**). | Vocabulary of travel and tourism; verbs describing impressions and feelings. | Describing your reactions to a foreign place. ✓ |
| 6 Travel:<br>A journey to the Himalayas | A running commentary. Listening for a visual impression of a place (***). | Asking for and giving information; making conjectures. Vocabulary of geographical features. | Planning and preparing a trip. |
| 7 Books:<br>The critic's choice | Radio panel discussion. Listening to three views of a novel. Educated, clear speakers (**). | Adjectives and phrases for describing books and films. | Describing a book or film you know well. |
| 8 Books:<br>A Sherlock Holmes mystery | A short story. Jigsaw listening. Nineteenth century English (**). | Language of speculation. | Solving a mystery. |
| 9 Buildings and cities:<br>A proposed development | Interview. Listening to descriptions of buildings. Clear informed speaker (*). | Vocabulary for describing features of a building; formal/informal register. | Presenting an unconventional design. |
| 10 Buildings and Cities:<br>A bid to host the Olympics | A news update. Split listening (***). | Language of speeches and presentations. | Making a speech in favour of a city bidding to host the Olympics. |

\* = below average difficulty   \** = average difficulty   \*** = above average difficulty

| Unit | Listening type | Language focus | Speaking activity |
| --- | --- | --- | --- |
| 11 Accidents: Common injuries | Interview with a doctor who describes a number of cases. Scottish accent (**). | Phrases for physical accidents; expert and layman's terms. | Telling an anecdote about an injury or accident. |
| 12 Accidents: Who is to blame? | Witness reports. Listening to first-hand accounts of three accidents. Some colloquial speech; mixture of accents (**). | Language of blame and responsibility. | 1 Judging who is to blame for an accident. 2 Discussing the responsibility for social and political problems. |
| 13 Trends: Social trends | Radio news report. Listening to facts about social trends. Dense passage (*). | Describing change (*increase*, *decline*, etc); giving reasons for change. | Talking about social and economic trends in your country. √ |
| 14 Trends: A crisis meeting | A business meeting. Listening to three people discussing a business problem (**). | Language of meetings and debate. | Role-play; deciding on the best course of action. |
| 15 Social English: Anecdotes | Monologue. Listening to an anecdote about a chance meeting. Scottish accent; fast idiomatic speech (***). | Narrative devices. | Telling an anecdote. |
| 16 Social English: Saying the right thing | A series of short statements and questions in everyday situations requiring a rapid response (**). | Short answers; everyday functional phrases. | Role-plays practising short exchanges. √ |
| 17 Humour: Just a minute | Radio panel game. Listening to four raconteurs. Fast, idiomatic speech; cultural references (***). | Verbs of joking (plus prepositions). | Game: Just a minute. |
| 18 Humour: Telling a joke | Listening to jokes and anecdotes. Colloquial speech (*). | Fluency practice. | Recounting a joke; devising a caption to go with a cartoon. √ |
| 19 The media: Newspapers | Monologue. Listening to a critique of modern journalism (**). | Vocabulary to describe news coverage. | Carrying out a survey on news reading habits. |
| 20 The media: Radio news | Listening to a news bulletin (**). | Passive reporting verbs. | Producing a radio news programme. |

\* = below average difficulty   \*\* = average difficulty   \*\*\* = above average difficulty

# Notes to the Teacher

## Introduction

This book is written for the advanced learner and is founded on the principle that students at this level have reached a stage where they can communicate reasonably well, but are frustrated by not having a range of expression which will do justice to the sophistication of their thought, and by a lack of a native-like naturalness. Although it is not always native speakers that they will need to speak *to*, they want to speak *like* them. Contained within this book, and on the cassette, are a variety of authentic listening and speaking exercises. In the recordings we have included as wide a range as possible of discourse types. They differ in content, from academic to anecdotal; in register, from formal to colloquial; and in accent, from mid-west America to British RP.

In the listening exercises we aim:

★ to develop listening skills experientially. We believe that the key to improving students' listening ability is through presenting them with texts which arouse their curiosity, because they are inherently interesting or because the accompanying task is motivating.

★ to avoid such arbitrary divisions as 'gist listening', 'listening for specific information', etc in the belief that at this level, when students listen to any text, they do so with the expectation of understanding it in its entirety.

★ to help the student towards a better understanding of the text through straightforward questions rather than seeking to test them or trip them up.

In the speaking activities we aim:

★ to generate genuine interest in the topic of each unit.

★ to improve, through the language boxes and vocabulary work, students' ability to converse naturally on a given topic (as opposed to merely expanding their passive knowledge of the language).

★ to provide generative contexts which allow the teacher to analyse and correct students' speech.

The book contains twenty units, each linked to a particular topic. To ensure ease of integration into a given course we have chosen ten topics which are commonly covered in most advanced syllabuses. Each unit is a self-contained lesson (varying in length from 50–90 minutes) with *substantial language input* and *skills development*.

A typical unit might contain the following:

★ a discussion that 'warms' students to the topic and the first listening passage;

★ vocabulary extension (related to the topic);

★ a listening comprehension task;

★ language work related to the passage;

★ a communication activity supported by a language box of key phrases.

# Some notes on how to use the book

One or two photocopiable *task sheet(s)* usually accompany each unit. Each one forms approximately a one-hour lesson, integrating listening, speaking and vocabulary work. Full *Teacher's notes* appear before each unit and you will also find a *tapescript* and *key to the exercises* there. There are however several general points to consider:

**Language boxes**

These are lists of key phrases which will facilitate the speaking task. In the Teacher's notes you will find suggestions on how to practise this language before it is applied to the main activity.

**Split listening**

This is where the class is divided into groups and each group is assigned a different task. All students then listen to the same passage. (Unit 10)

**Jigsaw listening**

This involves two groups listening to *different* passages from the tape or CD and then pooling their information. Consequently, in each case the relevant section of the listening material needs to be copied onto a separate tape before the lesson. (Units 8, 18)

**Remedial work**

It is assumed that at this level speaking to improve fluency is not the sole aim and that the teacher will therefore monitor all speaking tasks for correction and comment afterwards.

**Listening tasks**

Generally we recommend one or two listenings for each passage, each time there being a different task involved. However, should the students require further listenings then the teacher should of course use their discretion.

**Preparation for speaking tasks**

It is important to allow the student adequate time to prepare for a speaking activity (we leave it in your hands to decide exactly how long). In some cases this may mean no more than a few minutes, but occasionally we have suggested that the student prepares outside the class so that the activity can be done the following day or week.

**Photocopying**

Most units consist of two task sheets and in these cases we would suggest photocopying them on both sides of one piece of paper. On some task sheets there are role cards or cards for games: instructions as to how many sets to copy and how to divide them are given in the Teacher's notes of the relevant units.

TEACHER'S NOTES **1A**

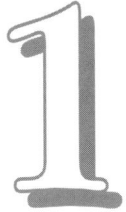

# People
## Jonathan King

> **Theme:** Describing and judging people's character, especially first impressions.
>
> **Main language points:** Adjectives and common idioms which describe personality; language to describe first impressions.
>
> **Listening type:** A radio interview with a pop personality (delivery clear, but rapid). Students listen for an overall impression of the speaker's personality.
>
> **Speaking type:** Students talk about someone they know well.

**Discussion**   Put students in groups to discuss the questions, having given them a few minutes to think about them. Then discuss in open class.

**Listening**   Ask the students to look at the nine words and quickly check in open class that they know the meaning and pronunciation of each.

Then play the tape through once getting the students to tick the adjectives which best describe Jonathan King's personality. Ask them to compare their answers in pairs using the expressions in the language box, and to justify their choice. They can come up with their own adjectives too, if they wish. Check in open class. Note: There is no one correct answer (except talkative!); the aim here is to stimulate discussion.

 Jonathan King interviewed by Claire Rayner

Taken from *Myself when young*, BBC Radio 2, 29 September 1992.

**CR** = Claire Rayner   **JK** = Jonathan King

**CR:** ... my guest this week, Jonathan King. You exude self-confidence, it's been said before. Were you like this when you were little? I mean were you ever shy or nervous or anxious?
**JK:** ...Yes, funnily enough I think I am still very shy and I've always been quite a private person and quite shy in many ways. I don't think it's actually self-confidence. I think it's self-knowledge, which is a different thing. I think if you have self-knowledge about yourself, uh, it's very difficult for you to get hurt by others, because if they're wrong who cares and if they're right you know it already, uh, and I've often had that kind of attitude so I think you know people criticize me and sometimes it's accurate and I go well yuh, I know that and sometimes it's wrong in which case well it's wrong and who cares.
**CR:** When did you get that self-knowledge, at what stage of your life?
**JK:** Um, I think probably later on when I was at Cambridge and I developed a duodenal ulcer and had to go to bed for about five months because the course of treatment then was you lay very calm and ate mashed eggs and mashed fish and nothing else ... (**CR:** And milk every two hours ...) ... and just let you cure yourself, exactly, and at that time I was doing all my revision for after exams and everything but also I did a lot of thinking about myself and uh working out what made me tick and what I was really good at, what I really wanted to do and so on. I think that was when things really got together because I then came out of that hospital bed and within six months I was number one in the charts and roaring all over the place and having a great time. Uh, it's something I would heartily recommend to anyone, to sit and think about themselves as early and as young as possible, because it's the only way I think that you can actually cope with the world and

# 1B Teacher's notes

everything else outside.

**CR:** Well how do you think you did think about yourself and who you were and what you were so young? I mean most children, I think, just sail along coping day by day don't they … (**JK:** Happily.) … or unhappily, as the case may be, but just coping with the days as they come? But you say you were thinking forward even then?

**JK:** Yes, I think even before I did that and ended up in the hospital bed thingy, I was. My mother was a very good mother, and gave me lots of very good advice. I remember, funnily enough I was talking to her about this the other day. I remember once she was taking me to school and I was six or seven or something and I said 'How can I get more popular at school?' because I was an ordinary boy and I don't think I was particularly popular, and she said 'Be interested in other people' and she said 'Now that's not as easy as it sounds and the way to do it is you start off pretending to be interested in other people and you make sure you say to them, "So how's everything going and how are things at home and so on."' And she said 'You know the most amazing thing will then start happening. You'll find that you actually do become interested in what they have to tell you.' And I did that and it worked like an absolute charm and two things happened, one I became overwhelmingly popular – I was probably the most popular boy at both prep school and public school – and secondly I found that I was genuinely interested in other people and have remained so for the rest of my life and I think it's probably the answer (to) why things like *Entertainment USA* become successful television programmes and yet funnily enough it very much conflicts with my public image which, you would think I'm not interested in anybody other than myself.

**CR:** What about with your brothers? Were you on good terms with them, were you as close to them?

**JK:** Yes, very good terms, and I think probably because of the thing of losing our father very early, I looked after my middle brother, who's only two and a half years younger than me, very much because I was always at school when he started so I would make sure that he never got bullied and was always looked after and so on and did so right the way through his school career. My younger brother who's much younger, several years younger, um, we just got on very well, like an older brother and younger brother, much more and almost a father/son relationship and he's grown up and as I said he now works for me and I have a terribly close relationship with him and his wife, who's a super girl called Jane, and my two gorgeous little nephews, one who's four and who's called Oliver …

Focus the students' attention on the gapped sentences and then play the tape again, getting them to listen for the relevant phrases. Pause the tape where necessary to give them time to write. Check their answers in open class.

**Answers**

1 *who cares/you know it already*   4 *be interested in other people*
2 *made him tick*   5 *not interested in anybody other than himself*
3 *coping day by day*   6 *on good terms*

## Vocabulary

Get students to match the adjectives with their opposites in the Listening section.

**Answers**
*quiet/talkative*
*thick-skinned/sensitive*
*sincere/superficial*
*outgoing/shy*
*thoughtless/considerate*
*modest/arrogant*
*unambitious/ambitious*
*demanding/easy-going*
*charmless/charming*

## Colloquial Phrases

Ask the students to decide what connotation each phrase carries, first giving the following example *He's his own man* and inviting them to say whether it is positive, negative or neutral. (*It is positive in that it suggests someone independent, principled and resistant to outside influences.*)

**Answers**

*He means well.* (Positive) This implies that although a person's efforts are not always

# Teacher's notes 1C

welcome or effective, he has good intentions; we often say this in someone's defence.

*She goes on rather/a bit.* (Negative) This implies that a person carries on talking unaware that the listener is tiring of listening.

*He doesn't give very much away.* (Neutral) This describes someone who for one reason or another doesn't let you know what he feels or what he knows.

*She gets on my nerves.* (Negative) This is simply another way of saying a person's behaviour irritates you.

*He's very easy to get on with.* (Positive) A common way of describing someone whom you find amenable.

*She doesn't mince her words.* (Neutral) In other words, a person is very direct, whether you like it or not.

*He's used to getting his own way.* (Negative) This implies both that a person is spoilt and that he doesn't find it easy to compromise.

*She's fine in small doses.* (Negative) This suggests that a person's company is something to be endured rather than enjoyed and she cannot be tolerated for long.

*He's generous to a fault.* (Negative) This means that a person is too generous for his own good.

*She's very down-to-earth.* (Positive) This means that a person is straight-forward, honest and has no pretensions to being sophisticated.

## Speaking

First get the students to choose the phrases appropriate to Jonathan King. Then get them to think of two people from the box whom they know well and to whom the language in this lesson might apply. The adjectives and colloquial phrases should be incorporated into a description of the people concerned. Students compare their answers with those who have chosen the same people from the box so that they can then report back to the class on which characteristics seem typical of a particular relative or acquaintance.

# 1 People

## Jonathan King

**Discussion**

You are going to hear a British pop personality talking about himself. **Before you listen, discuss these questions.**

★ Think of a public figure that you admire. What is it about this person that you admire?

★ Would you say that you had more than a superficial understanding of this person's character?

★ Do you believe that the true person is hiding beneath the surface in all of us? Or do you think what we see is the true picture?

**Listening**

As you listen to the interview with Jonathan King, tick (✓) the adjectives below which you think describe his personality.

- talkative ☐
- arrogant ☐
- easy-going ☐
- ambitious ☐
- sensitive ☐
- superficial ☐
- shy ☐
- considerate ☐
- charming ☐

Now discuss your impressions of Jonathan King with your partner, using the language box below to help you. Use any other adjectives you think appropriate.

---

**Talking about first impressions of people**

I found him quite/pretty/a bit …

He struck me as being …

He seemed/sounded rather …

He came over as …

I got the impression that he …

---

© David Briggs, Paul Dummett 1995. Published by Heinemann English Language Teaching. This sheet may be photocopied and used within the class.

TASK SHEET **1B**

🔊 **Listen again and use what is actually said to complete the statements below.**

1 He isn't easily hurt by what others say about him because 'if they're wrong _____ _____ and if they're right _____ _____.'

2 While he was ill, he thought about himself trying to work out 'what _____ _____.'

3 According to the interviewer, most children just sail along '_____ _____.'

4 In order for him to become more popular his mother advised him to '_____ _____.'

5 His public image is of a person who is '_____ _____.'

6 The interviewer asks him if he was '_____' with his brothers.

## Vocabulary

The adjectives below describe characteristics which contrast with the adjectives in the Listening section. **Find the contrasting pairs.**

quiet _____        modest _____

thick-skinned _____    unambitious _____

sincere _____      demanding _____

outgoing _____     charmless _____

thoughtless _____

## Colloquial Phrases

**Look at these colloquial phrases used to describe people and decide whether each has a positive or negative connotation or is neutral.**

He means well.                    She doesn't mince her words.

She goes on rather/a bit.         He's used to getting his own way.

He doesn't give very much away.   She's fine in small doses.

She gets on my nerves.            He's generous to a fault.

He's very easy to get on with.    She's very down-to-earth.

## Speaking

**Look at the colloquial phrases again. Which phrases could apply to Jonathan King?**

**Now choose two people from the box below whom you know well and whom you could describe with some of the adjectives and colloquial phrases from this lesson.**

| brother or sister | nephew | grandmother |
| local shopkeeper | landlord/landlady | boss |
| classmate (Be careful!) | doctor | neighbour |

**Find students who have chosen the same people from the box. Compare your descriptions.** Are there any characteristics that are common to each type?

PHOTOCOPIABLE

© David Briggs, Paul Dummett 1995. Published by Heinemann English Language Teaching. This sheet may be photocopied and used within the class.

**2A** Teacher's notes

# People
## Personality quiz

> **Theme:** Getting to know someone.
>
> **Main language points:** Adjective-noun word building; vices and virtues.
>
> **Listening type:** Students listen to someone answering a personality questionnaire on radio and fill in the questionnaire. The interviewee speaks with a strong regional accent.
>
> **Speaking type:** Students question each other in pairs about their tastes, attitudes and aspirations.

### Vocabulary and Discussion

Before handing out the worksheet explain about the Seven Deadly Sins and the Seven Cardinal Virtues.* Get the students to guess as many of these as possible. Then give out the worksheet and get them to check their lists against the real lists. Check that they can form the adjectives of these nouns (where possible): *slothful, proud, gluttonous, envious, lustful, covetous, angry; faithful, hopeful, charitable, just, prudent*. Students discuss the vices and virtues in pairs. Then get feedback in open class to see if there is any consensus of opinion.

### Listening and Speaking

Focus the students' attention on the questionnaire and check that they understand all the questions. Tell them to fill in the interviewee's answers as they listen. Play the tape.

 Personality quiz

**JW** = Janet Weir   **SH** = Steve Hurley

**JW:** ... (music fades) ... So, Steve, if you're ready, we'll get on with the quiz. (**SH:** Sure, fire away.) OK. Which living person do you most admire?
**SH:** My father and mother.
**JW:** And which living person do you most despise?
**SH:** My agent. Harry, if you're listening, I didn't mean that.
**JW:** What's your idea of perfect happiness?
**SH:** Oooh. Being curled up on a comfy sofa sipping a glass of Irish malt and reading a good thriller.
**JW:** What trait do you most admire in others?
**SH:** Integrity.
**JW:** And what trait do you most deplore in others?
**SH:** Sexual discrimination and racial intolerance.
**JW:** What do you consider the most overrated virtue?
**SH:** Hmm ... Thrift.
**JW:** What talent would you most like to have?
**SH:** I'd like to be able to strike a volley from 30 yards and see it rocket into the left-hand corner.

*The Seven Deadly Sins can be found listed in the writings of several theologians of the early Christian church, including St Thomas Aquinas. Committing any of the sins was believed to result in damnation in hell. The Seven Cardinal Virtues, which include the three basic theological virtues of faith, hope and charity, were coined later.

**JW:** What makes you most afraid?
**SH:** That I might wake up one day and find that all my success has been a dream.
**JW:** What word or phrase do you most overuse?
**SH:** Great.
**JW:** What's your favourite smell?
**SH:** The smell of a good fry-up wafting upstairs on a Sunday morning.
**JW:** OK. What is your favourite journey?
**SH:** Going home to Tranmere from London. When I see the docks on the Mersey, I have been known to become delirious with joy.
**JW:** When and where were you happiest?
**SH:** At the birth of my first child and at the BAFTA awards in 1990.
**JW:** How would you like to be remembered?
**SH:** As someone who did better than anyone, except his parents and his English teacher, ever thought possible.

Get the students to compare their answers in pairs. Then go through them in open class and ask them what they now know about Steve Hurley.

**Answers**

*He writes plays for the stage and for TV (BAFTA = The British Association of Film and TV Awards) and comes from a working-class background. He is a home-loving family man who likes football and the occasional drink. There is a hint of insecurity when he worries about his success being fragile.*

Students now use the questionnaire to interview each other. Afterwards ask them if anything they learnt about their partner surprised them. As a follow-up, ask them to interview someone outside the class, for example another teacher, a student from another group, etc.

# 2 People

## Personality quiz

**Vocabulary and Discussion**

**Of the traditional virtues and vices below which do you consider:**

☆ the least important virtue?    ☆ the most important virtue?

☆ the most forgivable vice?    ☆ the least forgivable vice?

### The Deadly Sins

SLOTH  PRIDE  ENVY  GLUTTONY  LUST  ANGER  COVETOUSNESS

### The Cardinal Virtues

HOPE  FAITH  PRUDENCE  FORTITUDE  JUSTICE  CHARITY  TEMPERANCE

TASK SHEET **2B**

## Listening and Speaking

🔊 You are going to hear someone called Steve Hurley taking part in a radio personality quiz. **Study the questions below and then, as you listen, make a note of Steve's answers.**

| Questions | Steve Hurley | Your Partner |
| --- | --- | --- |
| Which living person do you most admire? | | |
| Which living person do you most despise? | | |
| What's your idea of perfect happiness? | | |
| What trait do you most admire in others? | | |
| What trait do you most deplore in others? | | |
| What do you consider the most overrated virtue? | | |
| What talent would you most like to have? | | |
| What makes you most afraid? | | |
| What word or phrase do you most overuse? | | |
| What's your favourite smell? | | |
| What's your favourite journey? | | |
| When and where were you happiest? | | |
| How would you like to be remembered? | | |

What sort of person do you think Steve Hurley is? Think about:

★ his job.

★ his background.

★ his interests.

★ his character.

**Now work in pairs and ask your partner the same questions, making a note of the answers.**

© David Briggs, Paul Dummett 1995. Published by Heinemann English Language Teaching. This sheet may be photocopied and used within the class.

PHOTOCOPIABLE

**3A** TEACHER'S NOTES

# Language learning
## English pronunciation

> **Theme:** Phonological aspects of the English language.
>
> **Main language points:** Phonological terms; practising rhythm and stress.
>
> **Listening types:** 1 Interview with phonology expert. Clear, informed speaker. Students identify the difficult aspects of English phonology; 2 Nine short extracts featuring non-native speech. Students match the voices to descriptions of the accents.
>
> **Speaking types:** 1 Students talk about their own languages; 2 Students read a poem.

Vocabulary and Discussion

Put students in pairs to think of examples of each type of sound. Go through their answers in open class and correct as necessary. Then, in groups, get students to discuss what they find difficult about English pronunciation.

Listening 1

Play the listening passage through once getting the students to note down the main difficulties.

 English pronunciation

**PD** = Paul Dummett     **IT** = Ian Thompson

**PD:** OK, so could you tell me first what any learner finds difficult about English pronunciation? Is there one particular thing um ... which is difficult for all nationalities?
**IT:** I think one problem with English is simply that we've got so many sounds; that if you look at the vowel chart of many languages, you get languages with as few as three vowels. Um ... as you know Spanish and Japanese are a fairly typical pattern with five vowels each plus a few diphthongs perhaps; eight, eleven is another common number, but English has got this huge vowel count. I won't put a figure on it because it depends on how you count them: whether you count the triphthongs like /aɪə/ and /ɔɪə/ as vowels or whether you consider them combinations, but we really have got a lot of vowels and ...
**PD:** We're talking now about standard British pronunciation?
**IT:** Well, that's another problem, of course. Yes, if we take RP as the standard ... British RP ... things like *bud*, *bed*, *bid*, *bad*. For many speakers of many languages these seem hopelessly close together and easy to confuse and I think another point is ... although we haven't got a desperately complex consonant system, we've got, we get quite cruel clusters of consonants at the end ... at the ends of words. Lots of languages seem to have clusters at the beginning ... and we have them in English: /str/ as in *strong*, /spl/ as in *splay*; rather odd ones like /θw/ as in *thwart*, /dw/ as in *dwindle*. But English has very tricky ones at the end like *judged*, *sixths*, *strengths*, some quite unusual clusters of consonants, many of which only occur in two or three different words. I think probably *lengths* and *strengths* are the only two common words, at least which have got /ŋθs/ at the end; and particularly having the /θ/ and /s/ following each other and of course – I should say particularly having /s/ following /θ/ is difficult, although I admit that even English speakers simplify them. Um, another thing I think is the stress, intonation, linking system, the question, the presence of the /ə/ vowel, the so-called schwa vowel, the neutral vowel; the distribution of that is quite tricky. I think speakers of, say, languages like Portuguese and Russian, which have also got a system where you have very heavy stresses on the stressed syllables and very light stresses on the

unstressed syllables and a tendency to lengthen the stressed syllables and to crowd in the unstressed ones – speakers of those languages find less difficulty, whereas, as you know, for French speakers um … it really is a challenge because I wonder whether any two languages could have a more different system of stress, intonation, length, vowel quality than English and French.
**PD:** Right, I see. And is there … we touched earlier on RP and so on. What is recognized now as the standard for English? I take it it's no longer RP, that seems to be the preserve of …

Check students' answers in open class and then get them to answer questions 1–3.

**Answers**
*Ian Thompson thinks the main difficulties are:*
★   *a 'huge' number of vowels;*
★   *'cruel' clusters of consonants;*
★   *stress and intonation.*

1 *Because they have far fewer vowel sounds in their language (five vowels and a few diphthongs).*
2 *Like English speakers, they also use heavy and light stress; lengthening stressed syllables and crowding in unstressed syllables.*
3 *It would be difficult to think of two languages which have a more different system of stress, intonation and vowel quality.*

Play the listening passage again asking the students to note down the words Ian Thompson cites as examples of confusing vowel sounds and difficult consonant clusters. Note: Be prepared to explain the meaning of some of these.

**Answers**
*Confusing vowel sounds* – bud, bed, bid, bad
*Difficult consonant clusters* – strong, splay *(to spread out in all directions, eg your fingers)*, thwart *(to prevent someone's attempt to do something)*, dwindle *(to decrease gradually)*, judged, sixths, strengths, lengths

## Listening 2

Focus the students' attention on the nine descriptions of different pronunciation traits and ask them to work in pairs to match each description to a nationality. When they have finished, play the listening passage, pausing between each speaker. As they listen they should confirm whether they distinguished the pronunciation traits of each nationality correctly. Go through the answers in open class.

 Nine extracts

1 My name is Michael Hughes. I come from Keady which is a small town in South Armagh, in Northern Ireland. South Armagh is just north of the border in Northern Ireland. Where I live is about three miles from the border. Although that's my permanent address, next year I'm moving to Paris to live probably for two years, so I hope I can still remember some French.

2 My name is Hikaru Nagano. I'm come from Japan. I live near Tokyo. I'm in England for a short holiday. Yesterday I went to London to see *Starlight Express*. It is a musical on roller skates. I enjoyed very much.

3 My name is Marco and I come from a village in Switzerland. At the moment I'm studying at a school here in Oxford, but I will return to my own country, and my work, very soon – next week in fact.

4 My name is Carmen. I am from the south of Spain – Cadiz. I study public relation and labour law. I finish two years ago. At the moment I am in England. I have been here for a … and I am going to go back to Spain in April because I am going to open a nursery with my friend.

5 My name is Christine Saulnier. I'm from Paris. I am a clinical research assistant and I come back to Paris Friday and Monday I return to my work.

6 My name is Jeremy Rogers. I'm British although my early years were spent in America – I don't have particularly strong ties with the States – now I work as the technical director on a computer-assisted learning project.

7 Hello, my name is Roberto from Italy. I come the north of Italy – Mantova, near Mantova. I am 33 years old and in Italy I... my job is accountant, but when I go back home I hope to change my job.

8 My name is Mohammed. I'm from Sudan. I'm working in the central bank of Sudan. Now I'm going to learn English because I want to have a degree in business administration. Next week I will go to Paris to get exam.

9 Hi, I'm Adam. I major in English Literature at Harvard University. When I graduate I'd like to move to the West Coast which is where my brother and sister now live.

**Answers**

*They speak with a very regular rhythm. – ITALIANS*
*They often speak with a nasal tone and find it difficult to distinguish between 'l' and 'r'. – JAPANESE*
*They pronounce the 'r' following a vowel sound strongly in words like 'before', 'heart' and 'father'. – AMERICANS*
*Their intonation tends to rise in mid-sentence and speakers confuse the English 'v' and 'w'. – SWISS and GERMANS*
*They articulate fewer vowel sounds and also find it difficult to distinguish between the English sounds 'p' and 'b'. – ARABS*
*The intonation usually rises at the end of statements (and they pronounce 'r' strongly). – NORTHERN IRISH*
*They swallow their words. – ENGLISH*
*When speaking English they often say 'feet' for 'fit' and 'cheap' for 'chip'. They also find it difficult to pronounce final consonants. – SPANISH*
*They soften hard consonants, produce unique vowel sounds and pronounce the 'r' from the back of the mouth. – FRENCH*

## Speaking 1

Put students into small groups to do this activity and encourage them to look back at the vocabulary at the beginning of the unit. Don't expect them to have a long discussion about it, unless you can give them time to research the subject. A useful source would be *Learner English* by Michael Swan (CUP, 1987).

## Speaking 2

Get the students to read the poem once through to themselves, silently. Ask them what the writer sees from the carriage as it passes through the countryside. Then ask them how it should be read in order to convey the movement of a train. Play the tape. Then get them to practise reading it in pairs and finally have the class read it chorally.

*From a Railway Carriage* by Robert Louis Stevenson

Faster than fairies, faster than witches,
Bridges and houses, hedges and ditches;
And charging along like troops in a battle,
All through the meadows the horses and cattle:
All of the sights of the hill and the plain
Fly as thick as driving rain:
And ever again, in the wink of an eye,
Painted stations whistle by.

Here is a child who clambers and scrambles,
All by himself and gathering brambles:
Here is a tramp who stands and gazes:
And there is the green for stringing the daisies!
Here is a cart run away in the road
Lumping along with man and load;
And here is a mill, and there is a river:
Each a glimpse and gone for ever!

# 3 Language learning

## English pronunciation

**Vocabulary and Discussion**

Look at the words and phrases used for describing the sounds of a language and try to give an example of each in English.

| | | |
|---|---|---|
| a long vowel | an unvoiced consonant | a diphthong |
| a short vowel | a consonant cluster | the schwa |
| a hard consonant | a stressed syllable | |
| a voiced consonant | rising intonation | |

What do you find difficult about English pronunciation, both as a listener and a speaker?

From *Sound Foundations*, © Adrian Underhill, IH Hastings, published by Heinemann English Language Teaching, 1994.

**Listening 1**

You are going to hear Ian Thompson, an expert on phonology, speaking about English. **Note down what he considers to be the main difficulties facing foreign learners of the language.**

Now answer these questions.

1 Why might Spanish and Japanese speakers find English especially difficult to pronounce?

2 Why might Portuguese and Russian speakers have less difficulty?

3 What does Ian Thompson say about French and English?

**Listen again and write down the words that he mentions to illustrate that we have:**

☆ confusing vowel sounds.

☆ difficult consonant clusters.

## Listening 2

You are going to hear nine different nationalities talking about themselves in English. **Before you listen, look at the descriptions of the pronunciation traits of these nationalities and try to match each description with the correct nationality.**

|  |  |
|---|---|
| They speak with a very regular rhythm. | JAPANESE |
| They often speak with a nasal tone and find it difficult to distinguish between 'l' and 'r'. | ENGLISH |
| They pronounce the 'r' following a vowel sound strongly in words like 'before', 'heart' and 'father'. | ARABS |
| Their intonation tends to rise in mid-sentence and speakers confuse the English 'v' and 'w'. | ITALIANS |
| They articulate fewer vowel sounds and also find it difficult to distinguish between the English sounds 'p' and 'b'. | FRENCH |
| The intonation usually rises at the end of statements (and they pronounce 'r' strongly). | NORTHERN IRISH |
| They swallow their words. | SPANISH |
| When speaking English they often say 'feet' for 'fit' and 'cheap' for 'chip'. They also find it difficult to pronounce final consonants. | SWISS and GERMANS |
| They soften hard consonants, produce unique vowel sounds and pronounce the 'r' from the back of the mouth. | AMERICANS |

Now listen to the nine speakers and check if you have matched the descriptions to the nationalities correctly.

## Speaking 1

**Briefly discuss the difficulties that speakers of other languages have trying to pronounce your language.**

## Speaking 2

**Below is a poem for you to read aloud. It incorporates a number of difficult features of English pronunciation. It has a regular rhythm and needs to be read quickly.**

### From a Railway Carriage

*Faster than fairies, faster than witches,*
*Bridges and houses, hedges and ditches;*
*And charging along like troops in a battle,*
*All through the meadows the horses and cattle:*
*All of the sights of the hill and the plain*
*Fly as thick as driving rain:*
*And ever again, in the wink of an eye,*
*Painted stations whistle by.*

*Here is a child who clambers and scrambles,*
*All by himself and gathering brambles:*
*Here is a tramp who stands and gazes:*
*And there is the green for stringing the daisies!*
*Here is a cart run away in the road*
*Lumping along with man and load;*
*And here is a mill, and there is a river:*
*Each a glimpse and gone for ever!*

*Robert Louis Stevenson*

# 4A Teacher's notes

# Language learning
## Learning vocabulary

> **Theme:** The learning of vocabulary.
>
> **Main language points:** Explaining and defining (the meaning of words).
>
> **Listening type:** A lecture (clear but dense); listening and taking notes; students complete a mind map or diagram.
>
> **Speaking type:** A sophisticated word game (*Call my bluff*) in which students invent false definitions of words.

**Speaking**

Put the students in pairs, A and B, and give Student A the word *glistening* and Student B the word *lanky* on pieces of paper without showing or announcing them to the others. Ask them to look up the meaning of the word in the dictionary and explain it to their partner. Each student should then write a sentence using the word just explained to them and then compare their sentences with another A or B student to see if their understanding is the same. Then discuss the questions on the task sheet with the whole class. (Note: If the words above are already known to your students choose alternatives, but ensure that the words pose problems in appropriate usage.)

**Listening**

Before playing the listening passage, focus the students' attention on the mind map and explain that they must complete it as they listen. Play the extract and get them to compare their answers. Then play it again, if necessary. Go through their answers in open class.

 What it is to know a word

**CS** = Clare Sparrow

**CS:** … is not in itself a desirable thing. So, how should we teach words? Before considering this point, it's worth reflecting on what we mean by knowing a word. Obviously we have visual recognition – when we hear the word we can also picture it in its written form; and we have aural recognition – when we read it we can also hear it being said. From this ability to recognize a word comes the ability to produce it, that is to spell it correctly and to pronounce it correctly. There may be variations in spelling and pronunciation – note the controversy about *controversy* – but the majority of words have one accepted orthographic and phonological form.

Knowing the meaning is a more complex issue. There are many words that we hear and more particularly that we read which we understand perfectly well in the context in which they are used, but which we do not use ourselves. We don't use them because they are not near to hand – they're filed away in less immediately accessible reaches of the mind. These words are said to be part of our 'passive vocabulary'. Their meaning may be more or less clear to us – we could provide a passable definition of, say, *wise* as meaning something like clever and experienced without necessarily feeling confident of knowing when best to apply it ourselve. Through underuse accurate application of such words becomes more difficult. To know the meaning of these words truly we must be able to use them appropriately in a variety of contexts. In other words the speaker must be aware of certain factors determining their use: how the word fits into the syntax of the sentence, for example whether it takes a particular preposition or verb form after it, such as the infinitive or gerund; with what words it naturally collocates - an example of this would be to know that you can deny something categorically but not admit it categorically. Also we must be aware of register - could we say 'I was a bit put out to hear that you are not going to place the order with us' in a business letter? Or similarly to your best friend 'I regret to inform you that our meeting will have to be postponed'? Awareness of connotation is also vital: *zeal* is enthusiasm to be commended, but a *zealot* connotes someone who has lost his sense of proportion, a fanatic if you like.

When we know a word in all these ways, it can become part of our active vocabulary. Whether it does or not hinges on having the right opportunity to try it out. It is the job of the teacher to provide opportunities which are inherently interesting and motivating: generally these will be situations in which students can refer to their own personal experience. Ideally students will constantly be asking, 'How can I use it?', 'Can I say …?' or 'Can I use … here?' They will be all the time pushing at the limits of a word in order to consolidate their understanding of its true meaning. The long-term reward is a larger vocabulary, the control of which has enormous benefits: it facilitates variety of expression and precision in communicating one's ideas, which is what, after all, most of us aspire to both as speakers and as writers.

**Answers**

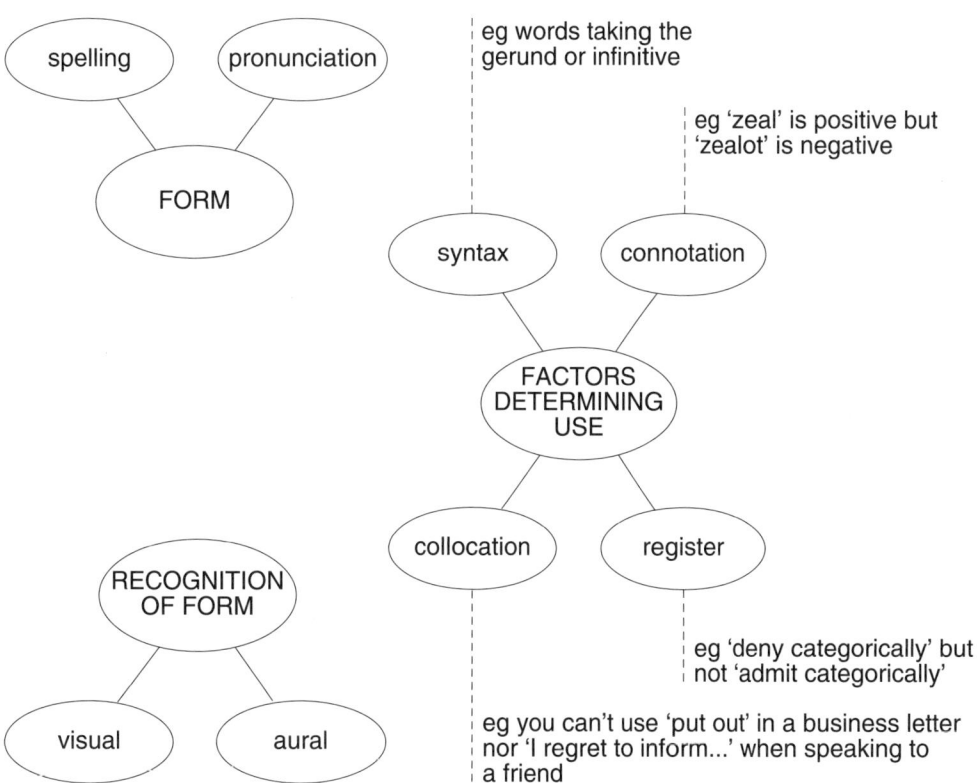

Call my bluff

Only give out the top half of the task sheet to each student and cut out as many sets of words as you need for groups of three to four students. Each group A will play against a group B. Ask them to read the rules and then give each group A one set of words (3-4) and group B a different set. Go through the 'tips' with the students and then leave them to prepare their false definitions. The groups then take it in turns to give the definitions and to guess the true one.

# 4A Task sheet

# Language learning

## Learning vocabulary

**Speaking**

Look at the word given to you by your teacher and think how best to teach it to your partner. When you are ready, teach it (without using translation). Now compare your understanding of the word you have been taught with a student from another pair.

Is your knowledge of the word the same as the other student. How did you teach the word? Was your approach different from other students? If so, in what way?

**Listening**

You are going to hear part of a lecture given by a linguist on what is involved in learning vocabulary. In this extract she describes all the elements that go to make up a full understanding of a word. **As you listen, list these elements by completing the diagram below.**

Now discuss the implications of the points made by the speaker for your own learning. Try to think of your own examples for each of the four determining factors.

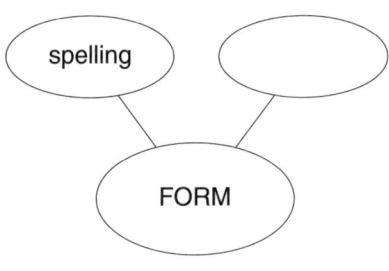

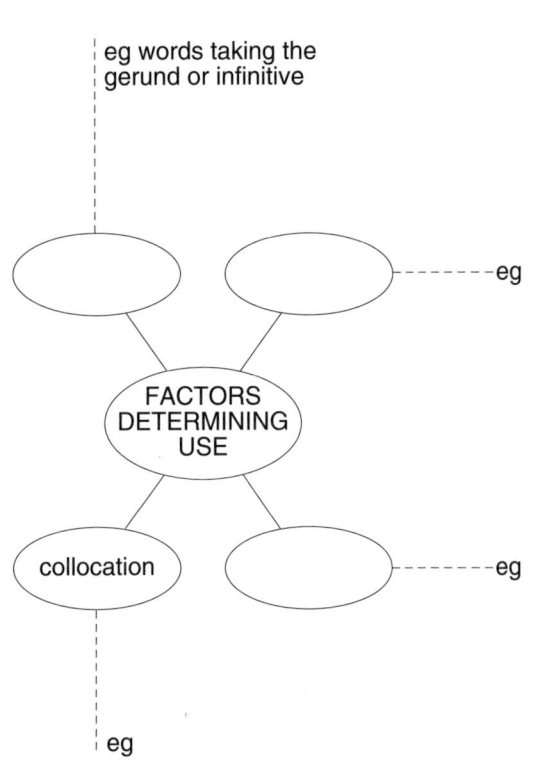

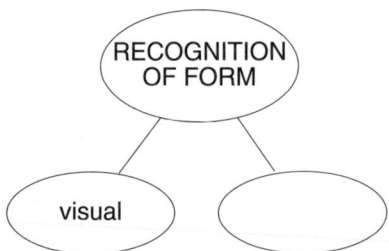

© David Briggs, Paul Dummett 1995. Published by Heinemann English Language Teaching. This sheet may be photocopied and used within the class.

# Task sheet 4B

## Speaking

This game is played in two teams of three people. The aim of 'Call my bluff' is to identify the correct definition of a word from three that you are given. If the team giving the definitions succeeds in misleading you as to the correct meaning, they win a point. If, on the other hand, you guess correctly, your team wins a point. Your team will now be given three words.

**Together prepare your three definitions. You will have to rephrase and perhaps elaborate a little on the correct one and, using your imagination, write the other two.**

*Some useful tips*

☆ Try to make all the definitions sound as likely (or unlikely!) as each other.

☆ Give examples to show how the word could be used in context.

☆ In the definitions the word could be a noun in one and a verb in another.

☆ Mention the register of the word; is it in current use?

☆ Think of the connotations of the word.

---

| | |
|---|---|
| **wince** *vb.* To tighten the facial muscles as if experiencing a sharp pain. You do this in response to unpleasant sounds, stories or embarrassing memories. | **withering** *adj.* Causing something to dry up or die; depriving something of its vitality; of a look, scornful. |
| **gobbledygook** *noun (uncount.)* The name for speech which, although spoken by a person in a position of authority, is actually pompous nonsense. | **drool** *vb.* To let saliva fall from your mouth without being able to stop, eg *The dog drooled over his meal.*; *metaph.* to look at something with lust or great longing. |
| **fretful** *adj.* To be distressed and anxious about something. | **doddle** *noun (count.) colloq.* A very easy task to perform; one requiring no effort. |
| **cranny** *noun (count.)* A small hole or recess in a wall or rock. Esp. in the phrase *nook and cranny.* eg *We searched every nook and cranny.* | **rife** *adj. (in a negative sense)* Widespread, commonly occurring; rife with treachery, corruption. |
| **slouch** *vb.* Not sitting or standing upright; adopting a lazy posture with the shoulders hanging down loosely. | **spittoon** *noun (count.)* A receptacle for spitting into; usually a round metal bowl with a funnel at the top. |
| **gust** *noun (count.)* A sudden rush of wind, air, snow, fire, smoke. | **bumptious** *adj.* Loud and self-important; conceited. |

PHOTOCOPIABLE

# 5A Teacher's notes

# Travel
## An American's view of Europe

**Theme:** Travel and tourism; impressions of a place.

**Main language points:** Vocabulary to describe tourism and impressions of a place; asking for and giving information; making conjectures.

**Listening type:** A travel writer's humorous view of Europe. (American English.) Students make notes on his impressions.

**Speaking type:** Students talk about a place they have visited and what they found curious about it.

### Discussion

Ask students to think for a moment about a good experience they have had when travelling and a bad one. Then get them to answer the other questions on the task sheet.

### Vocabulary 1

Put the students in pairs to match the vocabulary items. Check their answers in open class.

**Answers**

teeming with tourists – overrun with tourists
unspoilt – not commercialized
built-up – developed
out of the way – remote

hospitable – welcoming
to get about – to travel
to watch out for – to be wary of
to pay an extortionate price – to be ripped off

to break one's journey – to stop off
to wander – to roam

### Listening

Point out that Bill Bryson is from America and ask the students to think about the differences between the European and American way of life. If ideas are not forthcoming, prompt them with suggestions: food, leisure, geography, buildings, etc. Set the two pre-listening questions on the task sheet and play the listening extract.

 An extract from *Neither here nor there*

The first time I came to Europe was in 1972, skinny, shy, alone. In those days the only cheap flights were from New York to Luxembourg, with a refuelling stop en route at Keflavik Airport in Reykjavik.
I spent the day [wandering] through the ancient streets of Luxembourg City in a kind of vivid daze – an unfamiliar mixture of excitement and exhaustion and intense optical stimulation. Everything seemed so vivid and acutely focused and new. I felt like someone stepping out of doors for the first time. It was all so different: the language, the money, the cars, the number plates on the cars, the bread, the food, the newspapers, the parks, the people. I had never seen a zebra-crossing before, never seen a tram, never seen an unsliced loaf of bread (never even considered it an option), never seen anyone wearing a beret who expected to be taken seriously, never seen people go to a different shop for each item of dinner or provide their own shopping bags, never seen feathered pheasants and unskinned rabbits hanging in a butcher's window or a pig's head smiling on a platter, never seen a packet of Gitanes or the Michelin man. And the people – why, they were Luxemburgers. I don't know why this amazed me so, but it did. I kept thinking, that man over

there, he's a Luxembourger. And so is that girl. They don't know anything about the New York Yankees, they don't know the theme tune to the *Mickey Mouse Club*, they are from another world. It was just wonderful.

Sometimes a nation's little contrivances are so singular and clever that we associate them with that country alone – double-decker buses in Britain, windmills in Holland (what an inspired addition to a flat landscape), sidewalk cafés in Paris. And yet there are some things that most countries do without difficulty that others cannot get a grasp of at all.

The French, for instance, cannot get the hang of queuing. They try and try, but it's beyond them. Wherever you go in Paris, you see orderly lines waiting at a bus stop, but as soon as the bus pulls up, the line instantly disintegrates into something like a fire drill at a lunatic asylum as everyone scrambles to be the first aboard, quite unaware that this defeats the whole object of queuing.

The British, on the other hand, do not understand certain of the fundamentals of eating, as evidenced by their instinct to consume hamburgers with a knife and fork. To my continuing amazement, many of them also turn their fork upside-down and balance food on the back of it. I've lived in England for a decade and a half and I still have to quell an impulse to go up to strangers in pubs and restaurants and say, 'Excuse me, can I give you a tip that'll help stop those peas bouncing all over the table?'.

One of the small marvels of my first trip to Europe was the discovery that the world could be so full of variety, that there were so many different ways of doing essentially identical things, like eating and drinking and buying cinema tickets. It fascinated me that Europeans could at once be so alike – that they could be so universally bookish and cerebral, and drive small cars, and live in little houses in ancient towns, and love soccer, and be relatively unmaterialistic and law-abiding, and have chilly hotel rooms and cosy and inviting places to eat and drink – and yet be so endlessly, unpredictably different from each other as well. I loved the idea that you could never be sure of anything in Europe.

When I told friends in London that I was going to travel around Europe and write a book about it, they said, 'Oh, you must speak a lot of languages.'

'Why, no,' I would reply with a certain pride, 'only English,' and they would look at me as if I were crazy. But that's the glory of foreign travel, as far as I'm concerned. I don't *want* to know what people are talking about. I can't think of anything that excites a greater sense of childlike wonder than to be in a country where you are ignorant of almost everything. Suddenly you're five years old again. You can't read anything, you have only the most rudimentary sense of how things work, you can't even reliably cross a street without endangering your life. Your whole existence becomes a series of interesting guesses.

Go through the students' answers in open class and then ask them if they agree with Bill Bryson about not learning the language of the country he was visiting.

**Answers**

1 *Luxemburgers – they didn't have any knowledge of American popular culture eg The New York Yankees (baseball team), the theme tune to the* Mickey Mouse Club *(TV programme).*

*French – do not understand how to queue.*

*British – do not know the right way to eat hamburgers or how to use a fork effectively.*

*Europeans – are intellectual (bookish and cerebral), drive small cars and live in little houses in ancient towns, love soccer, are unmaterialistic and law-abiding, have chilly hotel rooms and cosy and inviting places to eat, and yet are different from each other as well.*

2 *He wanted everything to be new, unknown and exciting, as if he were a child.*

Play the extract again stopping if necessary to give students time to write their answers to the rest of the questions. Check in pairs and then open class.

## 5C Teacher's notes

**Answers**

3 *He had never considered it a possibility.*
4 *He had only seen people wearing them for comic effect.*
5 *He is used to doing all his shopping at one store, where shopping bags are always provided. Nor has he ever seen a butcher's display of unprepared meat.*
6 *He suggests that windmills were built to improve the look of an otherwise boring landscape.*
7 *This everyday activity has become a dangerous event.*

Play the extract again if necessary to enable students to complete the sentences.

**Suggested answers**

1 *It's difficult to take a politician seriously who appears on pop music videos.*
2 *I love Chinese food, but I just cannot get the hang of using chopsticks.*
3 *In order to speak the language well, it's necessary to have a good grasp of its grammar.*
4 *It defeats the purpose of travelling, if you are not prepared to try new things.*
5 *Let me give you a tip about getting about in my country. Never rely on trains being on time.*

### Vocabulary 2

Ask the students to add the correct preposition to each adjective or verb. After checking their answers get them to complete the passage with the correct phrases.

**Answers**

*to get used* to
*to be amazed* at
*to be shocked* by/at
*to be impressed* by/with
*to be struck* by
*to be apprehensive* about
*to be (un)familiar* with
*to be intrigued* by/with

*Coming from a small rural town as I do, I had been* apprehensive *about moving to a large city like London. In fact I was* amazed *at how quickly I* got used *to it. Although I was* unfamiliar *with the fast pace of life, it excited me and I wanted to be part of it. I was* struck/impressed *by people's energy and their ability to cram into a day as much as I would normally have done in a week. However, I missed the sense of community that you get in a small town and was rather* shocked *by the lack of interest or care which people generally showed for one another. At the same time the place held a strange fascination for me. I was* intrigued *by the extraordinary mixture of people that you saw on any day.*

### Speaking

Now give students five minutes to prepare an account of a place they have visited. Put them in groups of three to four to discuss their experiences. When they have finished get them to report back on anything interesting they heard.

TASK SHEET **5A**

# Travel

## An American's view of Europe

Discussion  **Think of one good experience you have had when travelling and one bad one.**
Do you enjoy travelling? What things do you dislike about it?

Vocabulary 1  Below are two lists of expressions commonly used when talking about travel.
**Match the words on the left with words on the right that have a similar meaning.**

| | |
|---|---|
| teeming with tourists | to roam |
| unspoilt | not commercialized |
| built-up | to be wary of |
| out of the way | welcoming |
| to break one's journey | overrun with tourists |
| hospitable | to be ripped off *(colloq.)* |
| to get about | developed |
| to watch out for | to stop off |
| to pay an extortionate price | to travel |
| to wander | remote |

Listening  Bill Bryson is a travel writer from Iowa in the United States. He first came to Europe in 1972. You are going to hear an extract from his book *Neither here nor there*. In this extract he describes his impressions of Europe and the Europeans. **Before you listen, discuss what the main differences are between people's lifestyle in America and in Europe.**

 **Now listen and find out:**

1 what struck him about

☆ Luxembourgers.   ☆ the British.

☆ the French.   ☆ Europeans in general.

2 why he did not want to learn the language of the country he was visiting.

 **Listen again and note down his comments about the following:**

3 unsliced bread     6 windmills

4 berets             7 crossing the street

5 shopping

© David Briggs, Paul Dummett 1995. Published by Heinemann English Language Teaching. This sheet may be photocopied and used within the class.

PHOTOCOPIABLE

## 5B Task sheet

The sentences below use phrases from the extract. **Try to complete each sentence in a natural way.**

1 It's difficult to *take* a politician *seriously* who
_____.

2 I love Chinese food, but I just *cannot get the hang of*
_____.

3 In order to speak the language well, it's necessary to *have a good grasp of*
_____.

4 It *defeats the purpose of* travelling, if you
_____.

5 Let me *give you a tip* about getting about in my country. Never
_____.

### Vocabulary 2

Below are some phrases which are useful when talking about your experience of new places. **Complete them by adding the correct preposition and then use the same phrases to complete the passage.**

to get used _____        to be struck _____

to be amazed _____       to be apprehensive _____

to be shocked _____      to be (un)familiar _____

to be impressed _____    to be intrigued _____

Coming from a small rural town as I do, I had been _____ about moving to a large city like London. In fact I was _____ at how quickly I _____ to it. Although I was _____ with the fast pace of life, it excited me and I wanted to be part of it. I was _____ by people's energy and their ability to cram into a day as much as I would normally have done in a week. However, I missed the sense of community that you get in a small town and was rather _____ by the lack of interest or care which people generally showed for one another. At the same time the place held a strange fascination for me. I was _____ by the extraordinary mixture of people that you saw on any day.

### Speaking

**Now describe a place that you have visited or lived in and say what struck you about it, mentioning any of its peculiarities.**

TEACHER'S NOTES **6A**

# Travel
## A journey to the Himalayas

> **Theme:** Travel and tourism; preconceptions of a place.
>
> **Main language points:** Asking for and giving information; making conjectures; vocabulary of geographical features.
>
> **Listening type:** A running commentary on a journey. (Some background noise and unusual accents.) Students listen to gain a visual impression of the places.
>
> **Speaking type:** With only a limited amount of information students speculate about what it would be like to visit a new place.

Note: The task sheets need to be copied onto *separate* pieces of paper.

### Vocabulary

Ask the students to say what the main geographical features of their region are, particularly those which make it an attractive place to live. Then ask them to work in pairs to complete the 'odd man out' exercise.

**Answers**
1 Oasis *as all the others are features of rivers.*
2 Glacier *as all the others are unpredictable land movements.*
3 Cliff *as all the other features have two sides.*
4 Pass *as all the others refer to the tops of hills or mountains.*
Note: 3 *A gorge* usually has water running through it whereas a *ravine* does not.

### Listening

Focus students' attention on the map and discuss what they would imagine this part of the world to be like (scenery, climate, habitation, roads and communication, what people do for a living).

Ask students to follow the speaker's route on the map and make notes on what can be seen at each point numbered on the map. Play the extract once through and then get the students to compare the information they have. Play the extract again, pausing it at the relevant points so that they can check their answers.

 **The Karakoram highway**

Taken from *Breakaway*, BBC Radio 4, 2 January 1993.

**BO** = Bill Oddie   **RV** = Richard Vaughan

**BO:** ... How about joining Richard Vaughan, trekking along one of the world's most perilous highways – no, not the M25, this is the Karakoram Highway, over the biggest mass of mountains in the world in north-eastern Pakistan? This road, which is notoriously susceptible to landslides and subsidence, and is therefore very dangerous, follows one of the ancient silk routes from China to the valleys of the Indus, Gilgit and Hunza rivers. Richard travelled it on foot and by Land Rover in reverse, just to make it even more difficult, I, when I say in reverse mean from India to China, of course.

# 6B Teacher's notes

**RV:** This is the Hunza valley which is so breathtaking, it's almost too perfect. There's an enormous river gorge below us, maybe seven or eight hundred feet, I can barely stand to look. The colours, it's er late autumn, and the colours of the trees are, it's like something by Turner; orange and red, just explosions of colour all over the place, yellow with green and the whole place, the whole Hunza valley is just ringed with peak after peak after peak, just these monstrous things.

This is Girelf village, I'm in an orchard, an apricot orchard on the banks of the River Hunza and as you can hear there is music going on; a festival is taking place.
**Man:** Yes, sir, animal festival of Aga Khan. Yes, sir.
**RV:** All the village is here?
**Man:** Yes, all the village is here.
**RV:** And I gather that's your uncle who's dancing at the moment.
**Man:** Yes, the locals are dancing here.

**RV:** Just above the village of Karimabad is the great monument of the Hunza valley, and that is Baltit Fort, some eight hundred years old it's reckoned. Now it's deserted. Until a few years ago it was occupied by the Meers, that's the rulers of this area. Forty-five years ago they gave up this fort. Today it's under renovation. It looks exquisitely attractive in its curiously stark fashion. It stands on a bluff which commands the whole valley and it was from here of course that the Meer, the ruler, could sort out any problems that were going on amongst his people.
**RV:** What is it we're looking for here?
**Man:** This is a place we get small pieces of garnet. The chance is that you become very, very rich and you don't have to go London.
**Woman:** You didn't just find those, you've been …
**Man:** Yes, yes I have.
**RV:** In his hand he's got a dozen deep red stones, the size of large diamonds. Wonderful. We're rich!

The sound of the Hussainabad river which flows down from the Hussainabad glacier curiously enough and we're just taking a little stroll up the valley here, strewn with boulders, pretty bare as most of these glacier valleys are of course, although if we look up to the left, there is a little cleft in the cliff face and high up there there are meadows where apparently there are shepherds and their cattle, certainly in the summer time.

**Man:** Yes, sir. There are living a lot of shepherds people up with goats, and sheeps and cows. They are making yoghurt, they are making fresh cheese, they are making the wool of the sheeps and goats, then who was our Hunza tradition of making caps. They are making lot of butter, sir, (**RV:** Are they?) we are using butter for winter time and for marriage time …

**RV:** There was a landslip there, did you hear that? Some stones just falling down ahead of us. It's alright.

**RV:** What about food and drink in an area like this?
**French girl:** The food it's better to avoid eating raw vegetables and unpeeled food.
**Tourist:** We've ate between 16 and 20 rupees for each person.
**RV:** 16–20 rupees, that's under 50 pence (**Tourist:** Yeah), that's 40 or 50 pence …
**Tourist:** Yeah, that's including the whole meal and *chai* at the end.

The three-hour drive from the lower Hunza valley, through the most incredibly stark magnificent scenery and the Hunza river turning to a most glorious blue, above the confluence with the Shimshal valley. The Shimshal valley, incidentally, one of the exciting places of this area, er, not so very many years ago raiders used to come down and er attack the caravans along the old silk route. But we have now arrived at Sost. This is the last frontier post before the Khunjerab Pass itself. A small village, but there are one or two hotels that I'm told are basic …

Thank you. So another checkpost, another barrier lifted. We're on our way again. The last leg now to the top of the pass and this is where the climb really begins. This is where we discover whether or not we suffer from altitude sickness. But now the gorge is beginning to broaden out and you can see ahead, although the gorge itself is in shadow. The afternoon sun is shining off the top of peaks that according to my map are something like 20,000 feet high. So even this far north of the spine of the Karakoram range, the mountains go on and on and on.

And at last here we are: nine hours from Gilgit, six hours from the Hunza valley, we've arrived at the top of the world it seems.

TEACHER'S NOTES **6C**

**Answers**
1 *Hunza Valley – breathtaking view of autumnal colours; deep river gorge and mountain peaks.*
2 *Girelf village – a festival of the Aga Khan with locals dancing.*
3 *Baltit Fort – a commanding view of the valley. People are looking for garnets (semi-precious stones).*
4 *Hussainabad glacier – a bare glacial valley. Above on the hillside are meadows where shepherds raise sheep, goats and cows for yoghurt, butter and cheese.*
5 *Shimshal confluence – stark, magnificent scenery; the river is a beautiful blue .*
6 *Sost – small village, one or two hotels.*
7 *Khunjerab Pass – valley is in shade, the sun is on the peaks.*

Speaking

Focus students' attention on the language box and go through the phrases in it, eliciting examples of how they might be used, eg I should think *accommodation is quite easy to find.* Put the students in pairs and ask them to speculate about a holiday in the Himalayas. When they have finished, they can do the same for any places which you would assume the group has a reasonable, but not comprehensive knowledge of, eg a nearby country.

# Travel

## A journey to the Himalayas

Vocabulary

Below are four groups of words each describing a class of geographical feature. **Circle one word in each group which does not fit with the others and explain why it does not fit.**

1  confluence      tributary       oasis           estuary

2  glacier         landslide       subsidence      avalanche

3  valley          gorge           ravine          cliff

4  ridge           pass            summit          peak

Listening

You are going to hear someone on the radio describing their journey along the Karakoram Highway in north-west Pakistan. **As you listen follow the route on the map below and at each of the places the speaker stops off at, note down what is happening and/or what can be seen.**

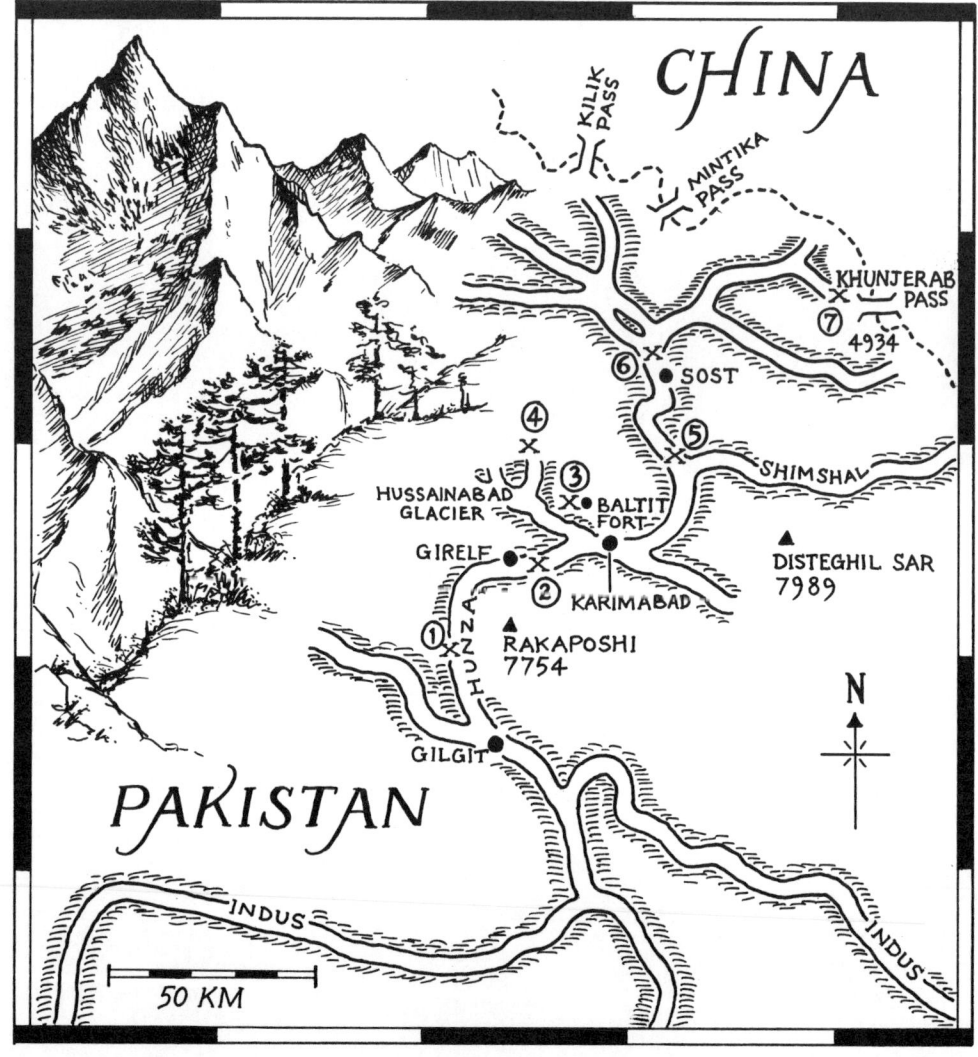

© David Briggs, Paul Dummett 1995. Published by Heinemann English Language Teaching. This sheet may be photocopied and used within the class.

TASK SHEET **6B**

1 _____

2 _____

3 _____

4 _____

5 _____

6 _____

7 _____

## Speaking

You and a friend have heard this programme (and may already know something about the Himalayas) and are thinking of taking a holiday in this area. **Using the language box to help you, discuss the advantages and possible drawbacks of such a holiday. Below are some points to consider.**

- ☆ accommodation
- ☆ possible dangers/risks to health
- ☆ getting there
- ☆ the language
- ☆ food/shops
- ☆ what to take with you

---

**Asking for and giving information**

Do you (happen to) know/Do you have any idea …?

*Question tags* eg You don't know if …, do you?

There aren't many …, are there?

I suppose/I would imagine/I should think that …

There should be/There's unlikely to be …

There's bound to be …

As far as I know/By all accounts, …

According to …

I'm afraid I have no idea./I couldn't tell you.

---

**PHOTOCOPIABLE**

© David Briggs, Paul Dummett 1995. Published by Heinemann English Language Teaching. This sheet may be photocopied and used within the class.

# 7A Teacher's notes

# Books
## The critic's choice

> **Theme:** Books.
>
> **Main language points:** Vocabulary and phrases for appraising a book and describing what it's about.
>
> **Listening type:** Radio panel discussion (intellectual speakers) of a new novel.
>
> **Speaking type:** Students present a book (or film) they have read (or seen).

**Discussion**

In pairs, get the students to tell each other what they read, what they enjoy and what they don't enjoy. Ask if they have read any books by American writers.

**Listening Part 1**

Focus students' attention on the categories in the table and ask them to fill in the details as they listen. Play the extract through once.

 *Beloved* by Toni Morrison

Taken from *A good read*, BBC Radio 4, 25 July 1993.

**MM** = Michael Meyer   **EB** = Edward Blishen   **TW** = Timberlate Wertenbaker

**PART 1**

**EB:** ... anyway between those you can walk into and those you can't. Michael, your choice.
**MM:** Well, my choice is an American novel called *Beloved* by Toni Morrison. She's a black woman – I think in her fifties – and it moves backwards and forwards in time, a little bewilderingly at first, but you soon get used to it, before and after the American Civil War. It's 1874 and a black woman called Seth in her late thirties lives with her teenage daughter Denver in a house that's haunted by the malevolent ghost of a baby. And we gradually learn that this baby was murdered by Seth, her mother, most horribly with a handsaw, and that Seth also tried to kill her two small sons and her daughter Denver at the same time, but failed. And then again gradually, like almost everything in this book we learn that the reason she did this was to save her children from the unspeakable horrors she'd had to endure and which she knows they would in time likewise endure at the hands of their owner, a white school teacher. Well one day a beautiful teenage girl comes to the house and gradually the mother and daughter realize that this is the murdered baby as she would be were she alive today. And this ghost says that her name is *Beloved* which were the only letters Seth could afford to have carved on her tombstone. At first Beloved is gentle, but she becomes demanding and then violent – can we blame her? – and Denver fears that she may intend violence to Seth or that Seth may again become violent towards her and so the story moves to its powerful end.

**PART 2**

I'd like to read if I may a bit from the book. ... 'During, before and after the War, he had seen Negroes so stunned, or hungry, or tired, or bereft it was a wonder they recalled or said anything. Who, like him, had hidden in caves and fought owls for food; who, like him, stole from pigs; who, like him, slept in trees for the day and walked by night; who, like him, had buried themselves in slop and jumped in wells to avoid regulators, raiders, patrollers, veterans, hillmen, posses and merrymakers. Once he met a Negro about fourteen years old who lived by himself in the woods and said he couldn't remember living anywhere else. He saw a witless colored woman jailed and hanged for stealing ducks she believed were her own babies.'

# Teacher's notes 7B

**PART 3**

I read this book first a year ago, and when I read it again now I found it even more impressive. I kept finding new excitements in it, as I will when I read it a third time as I shall.
**EB:** Yes, I must say no book has made me so bitterly ashamed of being white than that book.
**TW:** Yes, it's an extraordinary book because it writes a history which I think has never been written, so that although it's a novel, I have the impression of reading this unknown history, the suppressed history, since most of the history we know of America is definitely white. And she's put a face on these faceless thousands, hundreds of thousands of slaves which we know as a category. Slavery in America – you know they came on boats, you know they were slaves and then they were freed and their descendants are there and we know so little and that precision and that feeling of touching these people is what I found very moving and very rewarding about the book, so that every woman, every man that is mentioned in this book has a face, has a name indeed. (**EB:** Yes.)
**MM:** I love the way she, I mean the book I greatly, a novel I greatly admire, marvellous book, is Gabriel Garcia Marquez' *100 Years of Solitude*. And as in that book so in this, the way the characters accept the supernatural as a normal part of life like flowers and trees, so that when the ghost appears they don't think it can't be a ghost, they don't wonder, they accept, they know that such things exist.
**EB:** Yes, among other things, I think the book is one of the best ghost stories I've ever read. There's a tremendous – especially towards the end, when it moves into a whole dimension of the imagination, uh that I think I've rarely known equalled, so you don't actually, as you say Michael, you don't actually say to yourself no doubts about ghostliness ever arise because they are irrelevant. The meaning of the ghostliness in the book is a real, a deep, a realistic meaning in fact.
**TW:** Yes, if you think of modern ghost stories where you get these ghastly things like the *Exorcist* or something, where the appearance of the ghost is so disgusting and unbelievable, she makes this transition so that there is a beauty and a wistfulness about the physicality of the ghost.

Get the students to check their answers in pairs and then go through them in open class, referring to the first section of the extract as necessary for all answers except the critics' impressions.

**Answers**

Author: *Toni Morrison*
Title of book: *Beloved*
Type of novel: *Historical novel and ghost story*
Setting: *America, before and after the Civil War (1874)*
Main characters: *Seth, the mother; Denver, her teenage daughter and Beloved, the ghost of the daughter she murdered as a baby.*
Basic plot: *Seth murders her baby daughter to save her from the horrors of slavery. Some years later, the ghost of this girl returns as a beautiful teenager. At first she is gentle, but she becomes increasingly violent.*
Main theme: *The horrors of slavery in 19th century America.*
Critics' impression of the book – the adjectives they use
Speaker 1: *impressive (not marvellous)*
Speaker 2: *one of the best ghost stories he's read*
Speaker 3: *extraordinary, moving and rewarding*

## Listening Part 2

Focus the students' attention on the gap-fill passage and ask them to predict what words could fit (without actually writing them in). Play the second section of the extract (twice if necessary) and then check the answers in open class.

**Answers**

*During, before and after the War, he had seen Negroes so* stunned, *or hungry, or tired, or bereft it was a* wonder *they recalled or said anything. Who, like him, had hidden in caves and* fought *owls for food; who, like him, stole from pigs; who, like him, slept in*

# 7C Teacher's notes

trees *for the day and walked by night; who, like him, had buried themselves in* slop *and jumped in* wells *to avoid regulators, raiders,* patrollers, *veterans, hillmen,* posses *and merrymakers. Once he met a Negro about fourteen years old who lived by himself in the woods and said he couldn't remember living anywhere else. He saw a witless* colored woman jailed and hanged for stealing *ducks she believed were her own babies.*

## Listening Part 3

Focus the students' attention on the questions in Part 3 and play the last section of the extract. Check the answers in open class.

**Answers**
1 *Twice and he is intending to read it again.*
2 *Being white.*
3 *That it helps the reader to learn more intimately about slaves as individuals, rather than as a faceless mass (as she feels slavery has been portrayed in history books.)*
4 *The characters accept the existence of the supernatural unquestioningly.*
5 *The physical appearance of the ghost in* Beloved *is neither disgusting nor unbelievable.*

## Vocabulary

Ask the students to match the pairs of words and to discuss any differences in meaning or connotation within a pair.

**Answers**
*predictable – unoriginal*
*funny – witty* (witty is clever and funny)
*sentimental – romantic* (sentimental suggests a shallowness of emotion and therefore is usually negative)
*boring – heavy-going* (heavy-going means not easy to read)
*thought-provoking – disturbing* (the first makes you think, the second makes you uncomfortable)
*compelling – gripping*
*believable – plausible*
*touching – moving* (touching is lighter)

Note: As you go through the answers you can use these examples to help clarify the meanings of the words.
*witty* – Oscar Wilde was a witty man.
*sentimental* – Hollywood produces a lot of sentimental films, especially for children.
*disturbing* – *Schindler's Ark* was a deeply disturbing account of the holocaust.
*heavy-going* – Not being that good at French, I found the original version of *Les Enfants Terribles* rather heavy-going.
*touching* – It was touching to see the little birthday card that my daughter made for me at school.

## Speaking

Focus students' attention on the language box and go through the phrases in it, eliciting examples of how they might be used, for example *It is set in Vienna just after the war.* Give them a little time to prepare their talk (it could be done for homework) and encourage questions afterwards.

TASK SHEET 7A

# Books

## The critic's choice

Discussion

Do you read a lot? When and where do you read? What do you read (magazines, thrillers, novels, best-sellers)? How do you choose what books to read? How persevering are you with a book, i.e. how much will you read before you decide it is not worth continuing? What sort of books don't you like?

Listening Part 1

You are going to hear three people discussing a new novel by the American writer, Toni Morrison. **As you listen the first time fill in the table below.**

Author: Toni Morrison

Title of book:

Type of novel:

Setting:

Main characters:

Basic plot:

Main theme:

Critics' impression of the book – the adjectives they use

Speaker 1:

Speaker 2:

Speaker 3:

PHOTOCOPIABLE

© David Briggs, Paul Dummett 1995. Published by Heinemann English Language Teaching. This sheet may be photocopied and used within the class.

## 7B Task sheet

### Listening Part 2

**Look at the extract from the book and try to fill in as many of the gaps as you can. Now listen again and check your answers.**

During, before and after the War, he had seen Negroes so _____ , or hungry, or tired, or bereft it was a _____ they recalled or said anything. Who, like him, had hidden in caves and _____ owls for food; who, like him, stole from _____ ; who, like him, slept in _____ for the day and walked by night; who, like him, had buried themselves in _____ and jumped in _____ to avoid regulators, raiders, _____ , veterans, hillmen, _____ and merrymakers. Once he met a Negro about fourteen years old who lived by himself in the woods and said he couldn't remember living anywhere else. He saw a _____ colored woman jailed and hanged for stealing _____ she believed were her own babies.

### Listening Part 3

1 How many times has the first speaker read it?

2 What is the second speaker ashamed of when he reads the book?

3 What is the importance of the book according to the woman?

4 What does the book have in common with Gabriel Garcia Marquez' *100 Years of Solitude*?

5 How is it unlike other modern ghost stories?

### Vocabulary

**Match the words on the left with words on the right that have the same or a similar meaning. Then discuss any differences in meaning between the words in each pair.**

| | |
|---|---|
| predictable | moving |
| funny | plausible |
| sentimental | disturbing |
| boring | romantic |
| thought-provoking | heavy-going |
| compelling | witty |
| believable | unoriginal |
| touching | gripping |

### Speaking

**Think about a book you have read and enjoyed and prepare to talk about it to your partner. Use the language box below and the adjectives above to help you.**
(Note: Remember to use the present tense when narrating the story.)

---

It's about …/It tells the story of …

It is set in … in/at the time of …

It is based on a true story.

It describes the life of …

It deals with …

It is a comment on …

You gradually learn that/become aware of …

It's an extremely well-written book.

What appealed to me about it was …

I found it …

I identified/could identify with …

It left me feeling …

---

PHOTOCOPIABLE

# Teacher's notes 8A

# Books
## A Sherlock Holmes mystery

> **Theme:** Stories.
>
> **Main language points:** The language of speculation.
>
> **Listening type:** A short detective story (19th Century English). A jigsaw listening in which students piece together information to solve a mystery.
>
> **Speaking type:** Students deduce the motives for a crime and solve the mystery.

Discussion

Introduce the characters. Then ask the students to look at the four exhibits on the task sheet and to predict what crime might have been committed. Draw their attention to the language box and encourage them to use the phrases in it. Note: There are enough opportunities for the students to use the language of speculation which appears in the two language boxes in this unit, so it shouldn't be necessary to practise them with extra examples at the beginning. However, if your students would benefit from extra practice, present them with the following situations:

1 You return to where you left your bicycle, but it is not there.

2 A car drives through a red traffic light.

3 A woman runs into the street screaming for help.

4 Your friend is half an hour late meeting you to go to the cinema.

Listening Part 1

Set the pre-listening questions, play Part 1 and then get the students to answer the questions in pairs. Discuss in open class and give the answers.

 A Sherlock Holmes mystery

**PART 1**

There was a tap at the door and the boy entered to announce Miss Mary Sutherland. Sherlock Holmes welcomed her with the easy courtesy for which he was remarkable and [ushered] her to an armchair.
'Do you not find,' he said, 'that with your short sight it is a little trying to do so much typewriting?'
'Mr Holmes,' she cried, 'you've heard about me, else how could you know all that.'
'Never mind,' said Mr Holmes, 'It is my business to know things. I have trained myself to see what others overlook. [But] why did you come away to consult me in such a hurry?' Again a startled look came over the somewhat vacuous face of Mary Sutherland.

**Answers**
1 *Holmes deduces that Miss Sutherland is short-sighted, uses a typewriter and that she left her house in a great hurry.*
2 *Her nose had indentations left by her glasses (pince nez); her sleeve was creased where she rested it on the table when typing; her boots, though similar, were not an exact pair.*

# 8B TEACHER'S NOTES

## Listening Part 2

Set the pre-listening question and play Part 2. Make sure the students find the answer.

 **PART 2**

'Oh, Mr Holmes, I wish [you would help me]. I am not rich, but I still have a hundred a year in my own right. I would give it all to know what has become of Mr Hosmer Angel.'
'[And what was this gentleman to you?]'
'[He was everything to me. He was my husband to be, Mr Holmes, but he disappeared on our wedding day.]'

**Answer**

*Miss Sutherland wishes to find Mr Hosmer Angel, to whom she was engaged, and who disappeared on their wedding day.*

## Jigsaw Listening A and B

Divide the class into two groups, A and B, and send group B to another room. The two groups listen separately to their half of the story and take notes using the table provided. They may listen as many times as they need to. Bring the two groups back together and pair each A student with a B student. Get them to piece together the events and to speculate on how and why Hosmer Angel disappeared. Again draw their attention to the language box and encourage them to use the phrases in it.

 **JIGSAW LISTENING A**

'[You said you had an income of £100 a year],' said Holmes. '[Where does it come from?]'
'Two thousand five hundred pounds was left me by my uncle in New Zealand, but I can only touch the interest. Mr Windibank, [my stepfather, that is] draws my interest every quarter and pays it over to my mother, so they have the use of the money just while I am staying [at home] with them; [when I marry and leave home it will be mine of course]. But I find that I can do pretty well with what I earn at typewriting.
I met Mr Hosmer Angel at the gas-fitters' ball. They used to send father tickets when he was alive, and when he died they sent them to mother. Mr Windibank did not wish us to go. He never did wish us to go anywhere. But when he [had gone] off to France on business, mother and I went. It was there that I met Mr Hosmer Angel. He called the next day to ask if we had got home all safe and after that I met him twice for walks. But when my stepfather came back again, Mr Angel could not come to the house any more. Mr Windibank didn't like anything of the sort, and used to say that a woman should be happy in her own family circle.'
'And Mr Hosmer Angel?' asked Holmes, 'Did he make no attempt to see you?'
'No, he wrote and said it would be safer not to see each other [until my stepfather was away again]. In the meantime we would write.'
'Were you engaged to the gentleman at this time?'
'Oh yes, Mr Holmes. We were engaged after the first walk that we took. Mr Angel was a cashier in an office in Leadenhall Street.'
'What office?'
'That's the worst of it, Mr Holmes, I don't know.'
'Where did he live?'
'He slept on the premises.'
'Where did you address your letters then?'
'To the Leadenhall Street post office to be called for. Mr Angel said he would be chaffed by the other clerks for having letters from a lady. I offered to typewrite them, like he did his letters to me, but he said he wouldn't have a machine come between us. That's how fond he was of me, Mr Holmes.'
'It is most suggestive,' said Holmes. 'Can you remember any other little things about Mr Hosmer Angel?'
'He was a very shy man, Mr Holmes. He would rather walk with me in the evening than in the daylight, for he said he hated to be conspicuous. Even his voice was gentle: [he had] a hesitating, whispering fashion of speech.'
'Well, and what happened when Mr Windibank, your stepfather, returned to France?'

TEACHER'S NOTES **8C**

 **JIGSAW LISTENING B**

'It is most suggestive,' said Holmes. 'So what happened when Mr Windibank, your stepfather, returned to France?'
'Mr Angel came to the house again and proposed that we should marry before father came back. He was in dreadful earnest and made me swear that whatever happened I would always be true to him. Mother was in favour and said she would make it all right with Mr Windibank.
'The wedding was to be at St Saviour's near King's Cross and we were to have breakfast afterwards at the St Pancras Hotel. Hosmer came for us in a hansom, put us both into it and stepped into another cab. We got to the church first and when the other cab drove up we waited for him to step out. But he never did. When the cab man got down from the box and looked, there was no one there. That was last Friday, Mr Holmes, and I have never seen nor heard anything [of him] since then.'
'It seems to me that you have been very shamefully treated,' said Mr Holmes.
'Oh no, sir. He was too good and kind to me to leave me so. Why all the morning he was saying to me that, whatever happened, I was to be true.'
'Your own opinion then is that some unforeseen catastrophe has occurred to him?'
'Yes, sir. I believe that he foresaw some untold danger or else he would not have talked so.'
'How did your mother take the matter?'
'She was angry and said that I was never to speak of him again.'
'And your stepfather?'
'He seemed to think that I should hear of him again. As he said, what interest could anyone have in bringing me to the doors of the church and then leaving me.' She pulled a little handkerchief out of her muff and began to sob heavily into it.
'[Leave the matter in my hands],' said Holmes rising.

Listening Part 3   Set the pre-listening question and play Part 3. Students discuss the answer.

 **PART 3**

'[Leave the matter in my hands],' said Holmes rising. 'I should like an accurate description of him and any letters of his which you can spare. Mr Angel's address you never had. Where is your stepfather's place of business?'
'He travels for Westhouse and Marbank, the wine importers, of Fenchurch Street.'
'Thank you. You have made your statement very clearly. Let the incident be a sealed book and do not allow it to affect your life.'
'You appear to read a good deal into [the letters] which is invisible to me', said Watson [when she had left].
'[Yes]. Not only [are they typewritten], but so is the signature. The point is very suggestive; in fact it is conclusive. I shall write a letter to the young lady's stepfather, asking him to meet us here at six o'clock.'
At six o'clock the next evening they heard a tap at the door.
'Good evening, Mr Windibank', said Holmes. 'I believe this typewritten letter is from you, [in which you agree to meet me here today]. It is a curious thing that a typewriter has really quite as much individuality as a man's handwriting. Unless they are new, no two of them write exactly alike.

**Answer**
*The love letters handed over by Miss Sutherland and the letter from the stepfather to Mr Holmes were written on the same typewriter.*

Listening Part 4   Give the students a last chance to say what has happened to Mr Hosmer Angel and then play Part 4.

## 8D Teacher's notes

 **PART 4**

'I have here four letters which purport to come from the missing man, Mr Hosmer Angel. They are all typewritten. You will observe that the [typed] letters share exactly the same characteristics as those in your letter, [Mr Windibank, or should I say Mr Hosmer Angel].'
Mr Windibank gave a violent start.
'To enjoy the use of [a hundred pounds a year, you took advantage of a girl's trusting nature, and her short sight], to appear as her suitor and keep off other lovers. It was as cruel, and selfish, and heartless a trick as ever came before me.'

**Answer**
*Mr Hosmer Angel was Mr Windibank in disguise. His motive was to keep Miss Sutherland at home so that he could continue to enjoy the income from her inheritance. She never realized the deception because she was so short-sighted and trusting.*

TASK SHEET **8A**

# Books

## A Sherlock Holmes mystery

Discussion –
A Case of
Identity

You are going to hear a story featuring Sherlock Holmes, the great detective, and Dr Watson, his friend and companion. The other characters are: Miss Mary Sutherland, a young woman; Mr Hosmer Angel, her lover; and her stepfather, Mr Windibank. **Look at the evidence from the case below and, using the expressions in the language box to help you, discuss what type of crime may have been committed.**

A pince-nez

Letters

A typewriter

A wedding dress

> He may/might/could have seen that …
>
> She may/might/could have been wearing …
>
> He must have known …
>
> She can't/couldn't have been …
>
> Perhaps/Possibly she was …

Listening Part 1   **Now listen to Part 1 of the story and answer these questions, using the language box again to help you.**

1 What are the three deductions that Holmes makes from the woman's appearance?

2 How do you think he arrived at these conclusions?

Listening Part 2   **Listen to Part 2 and find out why Miss Sutherland is seeking Sherlock Holmes' help?**

© David Briggs, Paul Dummett 1995. Published by Heinemann English Language Teaching. This sheet may be photocopied and used within the class.

## 8B Task sheet

**Jigsaw Listening A and B**

**Listen separately to the two halves of the story and note down any details which you think are relevant in the table below.**

**Student A**

The situation of Miss Sutherland

The relationship with Mr Angel

The attitude of Mr Windibank

How the lovers communicated

A description of Mr Angel


**Student B**

The marriage proposal

The events of the wedding day

The reaction of Miss Sutherland

Her mother's reaction

Mr Windibank's reaction

**When you are ready, exchange information with your partner and, using both language boxes to help you, speculate on the disappearance of Mr Hosmer Angel.**

> Surely he wouldn't have …, if he had …
> 
> He might well have …
> 
> It's quite likely that …
> 
> It's just possible that …
> 
> I (very much) doubt whether …
> 
> That seems rather unlikely.
> 
> That's a bit far-fetched.

**Listening Part 3**

**Listen to Part 3 of the story and find out what the significance of the letter from Mr Windibank is.**

**Listening Part 4 – The solution!**

**What do you think has happened to Mr Hosmer Angel? Listen to see if you are correct.**

PHOTOCOPIABLE

© David Briggs, Paul Dummett 1995. Published by Heinemann English Language Teaching. This sheet may be photocopied and used within the class.

TEACHER'S NOTES **9A**

# Buildings and cities
## A proposed development

> **Theme:** Buildings.
>
> **Main language points:** Vocabulary and phrases for describing buildings; recognizing formal and informal register.
>
> **Listening type:** An interview with a knowledgeable and articulate local historian about architecture. Students listen to gain a visual impression of a building.
>
> **Speaking type:** Students discuss the characteristics of certain types of building and propose an unconventional design.

Discussion    Get students to talk briefly in groups of three about the buildings in their home town or area. Then give the same groups three minutes to think of types of house and typical features, for example *cottage, detached, semi-detached, terraced, mansion, block of flats, bungalow, four-storey house, thatched roof, flat roof, pitched roof, skylight, dormer window, french windows, shutters, balcony, veranda, chimney, affluent, run-down, residential, suburban*, etc. Use the pictures on the task sheet to illustrate the meanings of these words, where possible.

Vocabulary    Ask the students to work in pairs to group the words into four categories. Do not tell them what these are, but let them work it out for themselves (*shape, style/period, appearance/impression, material*). Go through the answers in open class, checking they know the meanings of the words.

**Answers**
Shape: *asymmetrical/pointed/curved/arched/round*
Style/Period: *oriental/Gothic/Victorian/classical/1960s*
Material: *brick/concrete/plaster/stone/tiled*
Appearance/Impression: *plain/striking/elegant/imposing/ugly*

Listening    Focus students' attention on the pictures and set the pre-listening questions. Then play the interview.

 Interview with a historian

**VG** = Vincent Gillespie   **DB** = David Briggs

**VG:** ...It's been a very interesting campaign in many ways, because one of the things it's done is bring people together to understand what it is that contributes to the special character of this area. It's a very mixed area – a combination of old houses, um, old institutional buildings, some of which were used by schools and other educational businesses, others which started off as car factories or printing works and which have now moved on to other uses. But the prospect of having a very high density student population, uh, transplanted into our midst has really made people reflect on what they think the special character of this area really is.
... One of the difficulties when you are building this kind of high density property in a residential

area is that not only does it usually have to be very high, but it has to often be very close to the perimeter of the site, and in this particular case one of the issues that we were very concerned about was the fact that the proposed building was coming within two meters, not only of the sidewalk, but also of the trees which are a major feature of that particular part of the area, and so we opposed the development in its earliest stages and when it went to appeal the planning inspector supported us and said in his opinion it was too dominating a building in relation to the surrounding properties. So although the result has been that we have actually got two phases of a hall of residence already built, the impact on the area has been mitigated in both cases by the efforts of local people.

**DB:** Right, so, um, the actual style of the building, I mean, what does it look like?

**VG:** Well, it looks like in many ways a cross between a farm barn and a kind of suburban supermarket, um, it's an architectural style that I think is alien to this particular area, um, because one of the features of an area like this, which is largely Victorian with some earlier eighteenth-century buildings, is that it has a very distinctive mix of vernacular urban architectural features, whereas the architectural style that the architect of this scheme has used largely draws on rural vernacular features such as hipped roofs*, dormer windows, um, red brick-banded patterning and very bright and rather sort of unpleasant orange roof tiles, none of which are really characteristic of the area. The other thing that we dislike very much is that most of the buildings in this area have slate roofs and pointed gables, whereas the style that this architect uses has instead tiled roofs and these, as I said earlier, these slightly unpleasant half-hipped roofs* that give a very bulky look to the roof line when you see it on the horizon. So we feel that it doesn't relate very sensitively to the properties that are already in the area.

**DB:** Right. But aren't there any other high buildings in the area?

**VG:** Well there is of course the Silesian College as it's called, which is a very striking middle Victorian building, built about 1866, um, but the thing about the Silesian College is that it stands in very clear open grounds, even though some houses have now been built in its garden. The Silesian College is 13.3 meters high to its ridge, but in fact it's relatively narrow and therefore it looks elegant and doesn't impinge too dramatically on its context – there's a good deal of open space in front and behind it. Now given the economic necessities of modern building, modern developers don't build like that; they try and cover as much of the site as they can. … So that this is really speculative overdevelopment and we've managed, I think …

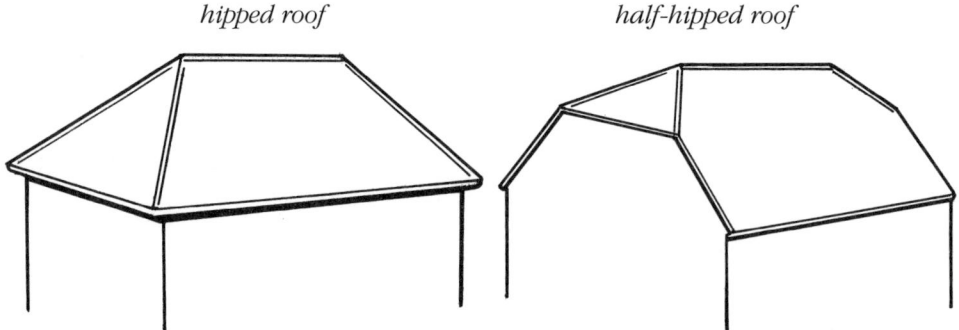

*hipped roof*        *half-hipped roof*

**Answers**

1 *Pictures b and e.*

2 *His objections are: too many students for the area; too large a building for its surroundings; the architectural style is incongruous (and ugly); it is based on commercial considerations.*

Focus the students' attention on the gapped sentences and then play the interview again, getting them to listen for the relevant words. Point out that the historian's language is more precise than is common with everyday spoken English and ask them to put it into more colloquial English.

**Suggested answers**

1 '… a high density student population transplanted into our *midst.*' – *a lot of students have been moved into our area*

2 '… an architectural style that I think is *alien* to this particular area …' – *a style of building which doesn't blend in with its surroundings*

**Teacher's notes 9C**

3 '… [the style of the proposed development] largely *draws on* rural vernacular features …' – *the features are typical of those found in country buildings (barns, cottages)*
4 '… it doesn't *impinge* too dramatically on its context …' – *it doesn't look out of place*
5 '… this is really *speculative* over-development.' – *they have built too much on the land to make a large profit*

Speaking

When the students have described the typical features in their groups, pool the information in open class. Now ask them to come up with their own designs, giving them enough time to prepare a description. It helps a lot if you, the teacher, can give a model of what is expected. Ask them to present their building at the front of the class. Encourage the class to ask questions.

**9A** Task sheet

# Buildings and cities
## A proposed development

**Discussion**  Describe the kind of building that is typical of your town. What about the area you live in and the house itself?

**Vocabulary**  The words below can be separated into four categories. **Decide what these categories are and then put the words into their correct groups.**

| | | | | |
|---|---|---|---|---|
| plain | oriental | striking | Gothic | brick |
| asymmetrical | pointed | elegant | concrete | Victorian |
| imposing | classical | ugly | plaster | curved |
| stone | 1960s | tiled | arched | round |

**Listening**  You are going to listen to a historian talking about a proposed new development for an area. **As you listen:**
1 tick the two buildings below that he talks about
2 note down his objections to the proposed development.

a  ☐   b  ☐   c ☐

d  ☐   e ☐

f  ☐   g  ☐   h ☐

The historian's objections are: _____

_____

PHOTOCOPIABLE

© David Briggs, Paul Dummett 1995. Published by Heinemann English Language Teaching. This sheet may be photocopied and used within the class.

TASK SHEET **9B**

🔊 **Now listen again and complete the historian's phrases below. Then try to paraphrase them.**

1 '… a high density student population transplanted into our _____.'

2 '… an architectural style that I think is _____ to this particular area …'

3 '… [the style of the proposed development] largely _____ rural vernacular features …'

4 '… it doesn't _____ too dramatically on its context …'

5 '… this is really _____ over-development.'

Speaking

Buildings conform to certain conventions. Schools, banks, etc are very much of a type. **Describe the conventional designs and architectural features of the following:**

☆ schools

☆ churches

☆ banks

☆ offices

☆ supermarkets

☆ hospitals

**Discuss whether you think these conventional designs are unavoidable. Work with a partner to suggest an alternative design for one of them and then present it to the rest of the class, justifying your ideas.**

© David Briggs, Paul Dummett 1995. Published by Heinemann English Language Teaching. This sheet may be photocopied and used within the class.

PHOTOCOPIABLE

# 10A Teacher's notes

# 10 Buildings and cities
## A bid to host the Olympics

> **Theme:** The attractions of a city (as a venue for the Olympic Games).
>
> **Main language points:** Language of speeches and presentations.
>
> **Listening type:** A news report (fast and dense). Split listening. Students pick out details of a particular city in order to fill in a table.
>
> **Speaking type:** Making a speech in favour of a city bidding to host the Olympics.

Listening

First pre-teach the vocabulary of speculating on the outcome of a competition: *to bid, to back, to narrow it down to, to put one's money on, to be in contention, a candidate, a (clear) favourite, a dark horse, an outsider, the odds are on*. Get the students to use the vocabulary by speculating about a current or forthcoming sporting or political contest.

Ask the students if they would like the Olympic Games to be held in their countries. In small groups get them to list the advantages and disadvantages it might bring.

Then give out the task sheets and ask them to study the notes on the five bidding cities. Check any difficult vocabulary. Divide the students into five groups and allocate a city to each group. Ask them to study the information and listen for the information missing from their city's profile. Note: It is important that you tell the students that the information *does not come in sequence*. Then play the listening passage (twice if necessary).

 Olympic bids

**EY** = Eleanor Young  **JM** = John McIlroy

**EY:** Excitement is mounting in the run-up to tonight's decision on the venue for the next Olympic Games. Let's go over to our sports correspondent in Paris, John McIlroy. Hello, John.
**JM:** Hello, Eleanor.
**EY:** Is it looking good for London? I have to say, as I speak to you, it's pouring down here outside Broadcasting House.
**JM:** Well, ultimately I don't think climate is going to be the deciding factor … but it's difficult to say. Obviously there are a lot of rumours flying about – most of which are contradictory – so I wouldn't like to say.
**EY:** Would it be fair to say that there's no clear favourite?
**JM:** Yes, certainly. This is what makes it so exciting. In the past, by this time, observers have been able to narrow it down to two or three bidders, but this time round all five are still in contention. Hence the great excitement.
**EY:** And why is that do you think?
**JM:** Well, there's no outstanding bid … with all due respect to the London campaigners … all five are perceived to have things going for them. And there are also some good arguments against them.
**EY:** What's the argument against London? Is it the threat of terrorist attacks?
**JM:** Well that's one consideration, but more importantly it's this old question of government support. … It's all very well the Prime Minister giving his personal backing, saying, 'Yes, we'd love to have the Olympics in London' and referring to the great British tradition of fair play and

sportsmanship, but the IOC is looking for cast-iron guarantees – in other words, solid financial backing – and so far the support pledged by British business, and in fact by the population as a whole, has been only lukewarm.
**EY:** Which country would you say has the strongest bid in that respect?
**JM:** Well, Singapore, I suppose. They've got the financial support. It's a wealthy country with a reputation for efficiency and reliability. What they haven't got is the Olympic pedigree of London, or for that matter, Athens who held the first modern Games back in 1896.
**EY:** Does that really matter?
**JM:** That's a good question – we'll just have to wait and see. What I do know is there are two strong, er, factions, if you like, in the IOC: the traditionalists who feel there's a need for the Olympics to clean up its act and return to the original ideals – recently there have been an increasing number of accusations of over-commercialisation …
**EY:** Therefore favouring London or Athens.
**JM:** … yes, and those who feel it's about time the Olympics moved away from the American and European continents and were held in South America for the first time or went to a Muslim bidder for the first time. I really don't know. I must say that the idea of the Olympics being held in a glamorous place like Rio has its appeal, as does the financial logic of the Muslim bid … After all, the Muslim world is one that the IOC would be foolish not to court. And Istanbul is anyway very popular with western tourists. But then again they might want to play safe, politically, as they did with Sydney in 1993, and go for the political neutrality of Singapore. That option would also mean less likelihood of dubious government involvement in the building programme.
**EY:** You mean allegations of corruption?
**JM:** Yes, I do. The IOC is anxious that the public image of the Olympics is not that of a huge money-making venture for certain governments and certain powerful individuals.
**EY:** This works against countries like Brazil or Athens, sorry Greece.
**JM:** Possibly. It's really a question of priorities though, and this is what's keeping us on the edge of our seats. We really don't know which way it's going to swing.
**EY:** And who do you think will be best-prepared if the decision goes their way. Who seems most confident?
**JM:** Well, I don't know whether this is a reliable indicator, but Rio are certainly the most active at the moment with eight different facilities under construction; needless to say, Singapore already has twelve state-of-the-art facilities.
**EY:** So, John, I have to ask you, who would you put your money on? It sounds as if Singapore is the favourite.
**JM:** Maybe, but I think it could be a dark horse, like Istanbul. They certainly seem to have learnt a lot from their previous bid for the Games in 2000.
**EY:** Thank you, John. We'll be returning to Paris for the announcement of the winner in our late bulletin at 11 pm.

After students have checked answers in their groups, go through the answers in open class so that they can fill in the information about the other cities.

**Answers**

1 *pedigree*
2 *state-of-the-art*
3 *efficiency*
4 *reliability*
5 *fair play*
6 *sportsmanship*
7 *Lukewarm*
8 *Prime Minister*
9 *attacks*
10 *2000*
11 *Muslim*
12 *Western tourists*
13 *modern Games*
14 *1896*
15 *over-commercialism*
16 *corruption*
17 *held in South America*
18 *eight*
19 *glamorous*

Speaking

Students *must* have adequate time to prepare their presentations. (It really needs to be done as homework for the next lesson). You can divide the speeches between two speakers or just leave it to one representative from each group. What is important is that all the group help with the written preparation of the talk. Give them ten minutes at the beginning of the lesson to put their ideas together.

## 10C Teacher's notes

As the speeches are delivered, the other students should make notes and evaluate them so that they can vote at the end. Encourage them to ask questions and challenge the speakers' claims. To avoid embarrassment, get them to submit their votes to you (in a secret ballot) and then you can write up the results on the board. Each first choice should be given three points and each second choice one point. (Use your vote to support the candidate with the fewest votes).

TASK SHEET **10A**

#  Buildings and cities

## A bid to host the Olympics

Listening  You are going to hear a news report about the cities bidding to stage a future Olympic Games. **First read the information about the five different cities. Then work in five groups to listen and fill in the missing information about one city.**

| City | Singapore |
|---|---|
| Population | 2.7 million |
| Climate | Hot and humid (30°C +). Heavy rains can fall in June and July. |
| Olympic history | No Olympic (1) _____. Has won one Olympic medal (Rome 1960). |
| Facilities for the 25 sports | Twelve (2) _____ - of - _____ - _____ facilities already built, more than any other bidder. |
| Arguments for | Strong government and financial support. Excellent telecommunications and infrastructure. Reputation for (3) _____ and (4)_____. Would provide recognition of significance of trading power of Pacific Rim nations. Political neutrality. |
| Arguments against | Lack of Olympic status. Less than ideal climate. |

| City | London |
|---|---|
| Population | 12 million |
| Climate | Mild and often wet (17–24°C in June/July) |
| Olympic history | Held games in 1948, despite national austerity after the war. Strong participation since first modern games in 1896. Fourth overall in medals table. |
| Facilities for the 25 sports | Eight existing, but most in need of modernization. Access often difficult due to traffic congestion. |
| Arguments for | Promises regeneration of run-down areas of city and to provide much-needed sports facilities for young people. Used to dealing with large numbers of visitors. Tradition of (5) _____ _____ and (6) _____ which are integral to Olympic ideals. |
| Arguments against | (7) _____ national support, even though (8) _____ _____ has given personal backing. Very congested and accommodation very expensive. Poor weather. Reputation for hooliganism, especially among football supporters. London a frequent target of terrorist (9) _____. |

PHOTOCOPIABLE

© David Briggs, Paul Dummett 1995. Published by Heinemann English Language Teaching. This sheet may be photocopied and used within the class.

## 10B Task sheet

| City | Istanbul |
|---|---|
| Population | 6.6 million |
| Climate | Warm and temperate. |
| Olympic history | Limited (31st in medals table). Bid once before for the Games in (10) _____ . |
| Facilities for the 25 sports | Only two existing, but good potential. Bid dependent. |
| Arguments for | Compact site. Multicultural image (spans Europe and Asia). First (11) _____ bid. Popular with (12) _____ _____ . The city has long wanted an opportunity to improve its infrastructure. |
| Arguments against | Traffic congestion. Poor telecommunications. Dispute with Kurdish separatists (thus possibility of terrorist activity exists). |

| City | Athens |
|---|---|
| Population | 3 million |
| Climate | Hot and dry (27°C in July) |
| Olympic history | Ancient games founded in Greece. First (13) _____ _____ held in Athens in (14) _____ . |
| Facilities for the 25 sports | Hosted European Games in 1982. Eleven facilities already built, some in need of modernization. Will be fairly spread out. |
| Arguments for | Great Olympic tradition. Appeals to those who believe that spirit of the Games needs resurrecting in the face of accusations of (15) _____ . Very popular holiday area with good accommodation facilities. |
| Arguments against | Very polluted and congested centre. Poor air quality. A reputation for lax airport security and recent allegations of (16) _____ . |

| City | Rio de Janeiro |
|---|---|
| Population | 11.1 million |
| Climate | Ideal conditions – warm dryish winters, temperature rarely falls below 25°C. |
| Olympic history | If successful, would be the first Games to be (17) _____ in _____ _____ . |
| Facilities for the 25 sports | Very few other than main stadium, but (18) _____ being built at the moment. Good accessibility. |
| Arguments for | Perfect climate. Is a (19) _____ city and has a vibrant atmosphere. Tradition of national enthusiasm for sport. Striking setting. |
| Arguments against | Problem of street crime. Perception of social injustice as money badly needs spending on slums on outskirts of city. International environmental campaigners have drawn world attention to exploitation of rain forests. |

PHOTOCOPIABLE

© David Briggs, Paul Dummett 1995. Published by Heinemann English Language Teaching. This sheet may be photocopied and used within the class.

TASK SHEET **10C**

## Speaking

It is the day of the decision. Before the IOC (International Olympic Committee) decide, they must listen to speeches by representatives from each of the five bidding cities, summarizing the arguments for their city. **Choose a city and then prepare the speech for it. Use the language box below to help you deliver the speech.**

**Opening Formalities**
Ladies, gentlemen (and members of the committee) …
I'd like to begin by …-ing (eg, thanking, saying, etc)
Before I begin, I'd just like to …

**Thrust of the Argument**
I'm (not) going to …
My/Our aim/intention is (not) to …
*Rhetorical question* eg What makes London …?

**Listing Points**
First/Secondly/Thirdly
In addition to this, …/Furthermore
As well as …-ing, … also …

**Contrasts**
Unlike …, London …
Whereas …, London …
Although …, we must bear in mind …

**Emphasizing**
I can't stress enough the …
Most importantly, …
After all, we mustn't forget …
*Stressed syllables and words*
eg It's not *if,* but *when* …

**Addressing the audience**
I'm sure you are well aware of the …
Needless to say, we …

**Concluding**
To sum up, …
I'd like to finish off/end by …-ing …

**As you listen to the other speeches, make notes and then give it a mark out of ten according to how convincing a case was made. When all the speeches have been heard, submit on a piece of paper your first and second choices.**

| City | Comments | Marks out of 10 |
|---|---|---|
| Rio de Janeiro | | |
| Singapore | | |
| London | | |
| Istanbul | | |
| Athens | | |

PHOTOCOPIABLE

© David Briggs, Paul Dummett 1995. Published by Heinemann English Language Teaching. This sheet may be photocopied and used within the class.

**11A** Teacher's notes

# Accidents
## Common injuries

> **Theme:** Accidents: everyday injuries.
>
> **Main language points:** Vocabulary and phrases for describing an injury and how it happened; also medical terms (awareness of register).
>
> **Listening type:** Interview with doctor (Scottish accent) who employs a mixture of medical description and anecdotes. Students take notes on the types of injury he describes.
>
> **Speaking type:** Students relate an incident which ended in injury.

Vocabulary and Discussion

Focus students' attention on the list of parts of the body and ask them to think of typical injuries that might occur to them. Use *tongue* as an example and elicit *bite your tongue*. In pairs they should describe the injuries in words or actions. Go through these in open class and then get them to complete the chart using the list of verbs.

**Answers**
Note: These are the most common collocations.

| | | |
|---|---|---|
| *graze* your knee | *poke oneself in* the eye | *twist/sprain* your ankle |
| *sprain* your wrist | *catch* your fingers (*in*) | *lose* your voice |
| *stub* your toe | *strain* your back | *bruise* your ribs |
| *pull/strain* a muscle | *bang/bump* your head (*on*) | |

Listening

Explain to the students that they are going to hear a doctor describing some common complaints and injuries he sees. Before they listen get them to predict the types of injury that are most common for each group of people. Then play the interview and ask them to take notes on the injuries actually described.

 Dr Ken MacPherson

**PD** = Pauline Doherty   **KM** = Dr Ken MacPherson

**PD:** What are the most common types of accident these days?
**KM:** Well you probably won't be surprised to hear that it's car accidents. Of course the most severe cases go up to casualty, but we see quite a few. A common one is people who, even though they've been wearing seat-belts and they've had head restraints they've still come in with a wry neck, in other words, a whiplash … from a collision.
**PD:** When you say a 'wry neck' you mean it's got sort of turned and it's uncomfortable for them to keep it, to hold their head straight?
**KM:** It's locked usually at an uncomfortable angle um and this is because muscles were strained or torn and have become inflamed and are now in spasm and won't allow any movement (**PD:** Oh, I see.) Um, well we do see some broken bones, twisted ankles – a lot of those. Similarly we get the results of domestic violence and we have to chart the finger bruises on the upper arm, the kicks, the punches … um quite often; the victims are generally women, but not exclusively. I've seen men with bad scratches, hair torn out at the roots, um black eyes … um …

**PD:** And do you see a lot of old people? I mean, I imagine they would be particularly prone to accidents.
**KM:** I don't think that's necessarily true. We do treat a lot of old people, yes, for leg ulcers, stiff joints and so on … and we do a lot of counselling, that's to say allaying people's fears about their, what they see as, their deteriorating health. Um … of course if an old person does fall over or bang their arm or leg on something, it's much more likely to result in serious bruising or a fracture than if the person taking the knock were much younger and had less brittle bones.
**PD:** Hmm, I see … And what about children? I did some pretty stupid things myself as a girl. Apart from getting my head stuck in railings, which I suppose every child has a go at at one time or another, I remember once putting a piece of dock leaf up my nose; I don't know why – experimenting, I suppose. Anyway, when I couldn't get it out with my fingers, I tried using a pencil and pushed it even further in – it was quite painful actually – I can remember my eyes watering terribly and a shooting pain. The doctor was quite good about it though; he just pulled it out with a pair of tweezers. Do you see a lot of those kinds of accident, you know caused through carelessness or just plain foolishness?
**KM:** With children, you mean? (**PD:** Hmm.) Yes, we do see quite a number of children who have inserted things into various orifices: noses and ears, things like peanuts and bits of bread. Quite recently I had a boy who had a moth trapped in his inner ear. He hadn't actually inserted it himself, on purpose – he'd put on an anorak with a hood and the moth had been inside the hood. He'd felt a loud buzzing in his ear and thought it was a fly. Poor chap, his friends found it very amusing; they suggested he put a spider in the other ear. It was wedged in so deeply that I couldn't actually see the moth and I thought his eardrum had burst. It was only as I was cleaning the ear that I noticed the tip of a wing and fortunately, as with your dock leaf, the problem was solved with tweezers.
**PD:** Amazing! Do these sort of things irritate you? … I mean, not perhaps that particular example but others you mentioned … I mean, they're really unnecessary accidents that could easily have been avoided?
**KM:** Not really, no. An accident is an accident. With children you have to assume a certain degree of carelessness that you don't expect from an adult. A certain amount of falling over and falling off things and breaking limbs is inevitable. But we do get people who are repeatedly harming themselves, almost for the sake of it. Somebody I remember twice within the space of two months had cut their forearm so their forearm looked rather like a joint of pork, with the skin scored ready for baking, um, and the same person, injected ink into themselves and had a blue arm. Self-mutilation is comparatively common.

In pairs get students to pool their information and then go through the answers in class. Then ask them to recount the incidents involving children.

### Answers
Adults – *wry neck (from whiplash), broken bones, twisted ankles, bruises; scratches, hair torn out at the roots, black eyes (results of domestic violence); cutting the forearm, injecting ink into the arm (results of self-mutilation)*
Old people – *serious bruising, fractures (from falls or bangs)*
Children – *inserting things into orifices, for example a dock leaf up the nose, moth in the ear, breaking limbs (from falls)*

Focus the students' attention on the gapped sentences and then play the interview again, getting them to listen for the relevant words.

### Answers
1 *strained/torn*
2 *generally/exclusively*
3 *prone*
4 *allaying*
5 *watering/shooting*
6 *wedged/burst*
7 *sake*

## 11C Teacher's notes

### Vocabulary

Introduce the subject of register with an example, eg *break* and *fracture,* asking the students which word a layman would normally use. Then focus attention on the ten expressions and get the students to divide them into two groups.

**Answers**
Layman – *a twisted ankle/a black eye/bad scratches/hair torn out at the roots*
Doctor – *a wry neck/orifice/muscles in spasm/inner ear/bruises on the upper arm/brittle bones*
Note: In the interview the doctor uses a mixture of medical and non-medical terminology because he is speaking to a layman.

### Speaking

Give students time to prepare and then get them to relate their stories to two other people in the class. Monitor their accounts closely and choose the more interesting or bizarre stories to be related to the whole class at the end.

TASK SHEET 11A

# Accidents

## Common injuries

Vocabulary and Discussion

Below is a list of various parts of the body (or faculties). **Using mime as well as verbal explanation, describe to each other the injuries which most commonly occur to these parts of the body. Do not worry for now about trying to put a name to each injury.**

_____ your knee  _____ your wrist  _____ your toe  _____ a muscle

_____ the eye  _____ your fingers  _____ your back  _____ your head

_____ your ankle  _____ your voice  _____ your ribs

**Now look at the verbs below and match them with the parts of the body above.**
Note: Sometimes there is more than one possibility.

> sprain   twist   pull   bruise   lose   catch … in   strain
> stub   graze   bump   bang … on   poke (oneself in)

PHOTOCOPIABLE

© David Briggs, Paul Dummett 1995. Published by Heinemann English Language Teaching. This sheet may be photocopied and used within the class.

## Listening

🗣 You are going to hear a doctor talking about the types of accidents his patients have. **The first time you listen, note down any injuries (not conditions) he ascribes to the following groups:**

_____

★ Adults

_____

★ Old people

_____

★ Children

_____

Can you recount either of the slightly unusual incidents involving children?

🗣 **Now listen again and complete the sentences below.**

1 '… and this is because muscles were _____ or _____ and have become inflamed …'

2 '… quite often. The victims are _____ women, but not _____.'

3 '… I imagine they [old people] would be particularly _____ to accidents.'

4 '… we do a lot of counselling, that's to say _____ people's fears about what they see as their deteriorating health.'

5 'I can remember my eyes _____ terribly and a _____ pain.'

6 'It was _____ in so deeply that I couldn't actually see the moth and I thought his eardrum had _____ .'

7 '… we do get people who are repeatedly harming themselves, almost for the _____ of it.'

## Vocabulary

The doctor, being a doctor, uses expressions that a layman probably would not use. **Look at the ten expressions below taken from the interview. Decide which five are more likely to be used only by someone in the medical profession.**

| | | | |
|---|---|---|---|
| a wry neck | a twisted ankle | a black eye | bad scratches |
| orifice | muscles in spasm | inner ear | bruises on the upper arm |
| brittle bones | hair torn out at the roots | | |

## Speaking

**Describe in detail two incidents from your childhood:**

★ where someone, perhaps you, was injured.

★ where you narrowly missed being injured.

# Teacher's notes 12A

# Accidents
## Who is to blame?

> **Theme:** Accidents: the responsibility for road accidents.
>
> **Main language points:** The language of blame and responsibility.
>
> **Listening type:** Anecdotal accounts of three traffic accidents (more colloquial English). Students translate the action described onto a diagram.
>
> **Speaking type:** Discussing who is to blame for a) the three accidents and b) social, political and environmental problems.

## Listening and Speaking

First pre-teach the vocabulary necessary for talking about car accidents: to run into, to crash, to run over, to knock down, to hit, to swerve, to skid, to be written off (ie unrepairable), a dent, a scratch. Get the students to use the vocabulary by describing a (minor) accident they have witnessed. Note: Be sensitive to the possibility of some students having been involved in serious accidents. Then discuss in open class how bystanders in different countries react to such accidents.

Give out the task sheet and focus students' attention on the language box. Describe the following situations and get them to use the expressions to say who is to blame: 1 You slip on an icy pavement and break your leg; 2 In a pub a landlord keeps serving drinks to a man who then leaves and drives his car straight into a lamp-post; 3 You run over a dog in the road.

Now ask the students to study the diagram. Tell them that they will have to mark the position of the cars, cyclists and pedestrians involved in the three different accidents. Play the listening passage through once, pausing between each accident (Note: Point out beforehand that there are two accounts of the second accident) and allowing students time to discuss what happened.

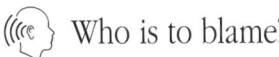 Who is to blame?

**GC** = Geraldine Charles   **TW** = Terry Walton   **LH** = Linda Hughes   **CC** = Charles Conham

**PART 1**

**GC:** I was on my way to work. It must have been about half eight in the morning and as usual there was a long line of traffic in South Parks Road waiting to turn into Parks Road. There were a fair few bikes on the road because the university students were starting to arrive for their lectures in the science area. That's what makes turning out of there such a pain – it takes ages. Anyway, when I got to the junction, I signalled right. There was a car approaching and he was indicating left, to turn into South Parks Road to go in the opposite direction from the one I was travelling in. And this is very common. There's almost as much traffic going that way in the morning as there is going the way I was and quite often you find two cars turning simultaneously – one into South Parks Road from the north and one out of it, heading north. Well, that's what happened on this occasion, except that the idiot who was indicating left, for some reason best known to himself, decided to go straight on and crashed into the side of me as I was turning. Luckily he caught the back door of my car and not my door or it could have been very nasty indeed.

## 12B Teacher's notes

### PART 2A

**TW:** I was waiting at the lights at the corner of Parks Road and Broad Street. It was a quiet afternoon. There wasn't much traffic on the roads. The road markings are funny because there are two white lines in front of the lights. One is where the cars should stop and the other is where bicycles should stop. To be honest, I never worked out which is which, so I always stop at the first one. The light turned from red to amber and I edged forward and, when I got to the second white line, I stopped momentarily. It was really an unconscious reflex … you know … having come to a white line on the road, which generally means 'Stop'. Anyway, the next thing I knew, there was an enormous jolt. When I recovered my composure I turned round and saw that a car had run straight into the back of me.

### PART 2B

**LH:** I was coming up to the lights at the end of Parks Road. I must have been doing about 25 miles an hour. There was a car waiting at the lights and, um, as I got nearer to it, the lights turned from red to green. This bloke, he edged forward as they turned and I let off the brake, assuming, you know, as anyone would, that he was moving off … because of the green light. So then what does he do? He suddenly stops. I mean, people do some stupid things but you don't expect them to do exactly the opposite of what the signal tells them. I braked hard, but it was too late and I ran into the back of him.

### PART 3

**CC:** I was on my way back to my office in the city centre from lunch, a little reluctantly, and I was going at a gentle pace. I make it a rule never to hurry to work. In any case, Broad Street wasn't built for Grand Prix racing, particularly the part I was in: there are cars parked in the middle of the street and you always have to be on the alert in case one pulls out suddenly. And what's more, cars constantly circle the parking island looking for spaces, rather like sharks, so one of these can also stop quite suddenly when they see a space. Anyway, umm, there was a cyclist slightly in front of me weaving about – he'd probably had a good liquid lunch too. I gave him a wide berth and made no attempt to overtake him. But the swaying motion of the bike dislodged a large bag which was perched precariously on a rack at the back and it fell off, right in the middle of the road. I swerved automatically to avoid it and veered towards the pavement. It all happened so quickly. Having avoided one obstacle, I found myself faced with another – a young boy was walking in the road, well, in the gutter to be more precise, and the front corner of the car caught his leg and, umm, sent the poor chap flying. Thank God, he wasn't badly injured, but it was a horribly close shave.

**Answers**

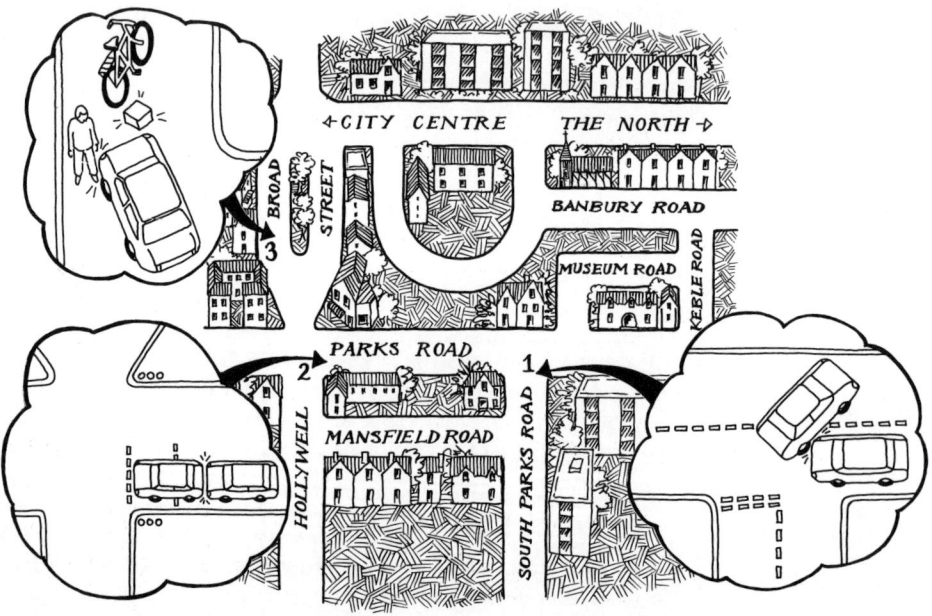

Play the listening passage a second time and get students in open class to give a full account of each accident. Then, in pairs, get them to discuss the responsibility for each accident, using the language box to help them.

TASK SHEET **12A**

# 12 Accidents

## Who is to blame?

Listening and Speaking

You are going to hear accounts of three road accidents. **As you listen, mark on the diagram below where the cars, cyclists or pedestrians were in each case.**

Note: In the case of the second accident you will hear two different accounts of the same accident, but in the others only one.

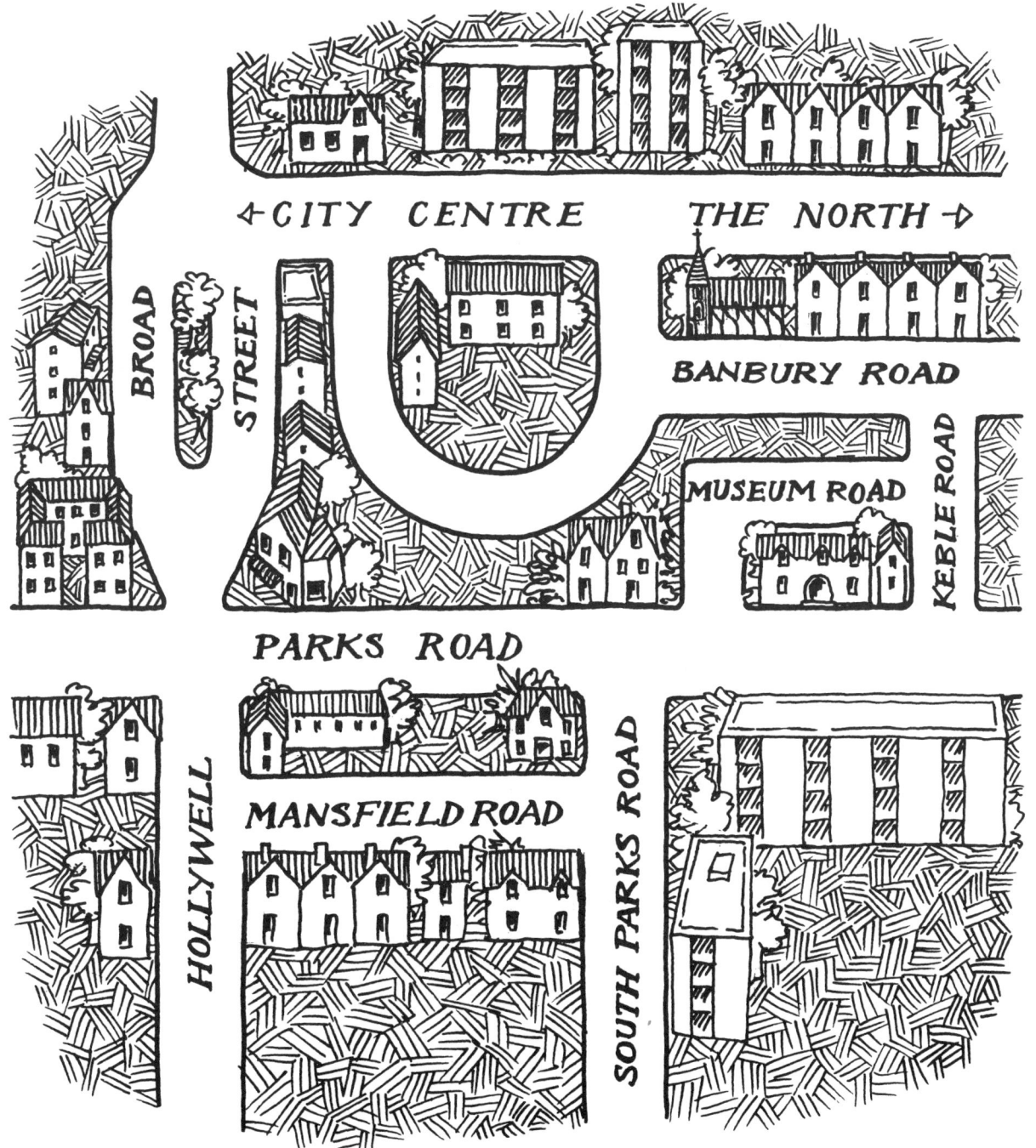

© David Briggs, Paul Dummett 1995. Published by Heinemann English Language Teaching. This sheet may be photocopied and used within the class.

PHOTOCOPIABLE

## 12B Task sheet

**Now, using the language box to help you, discuss who you think is to blame for each accident.**

> He is to blame.
>
> He is chiefly/in part to blame for (not) …-ing.
>
> It's his fault.
>
> The fault/responsibility lies with the person who …
>
> It had nothing to do with her/the fact that …
>
> It was (entirely) his own fault.
>
> It serves him right (for not …-ing).
>
> He was guilty of … (eg negligence).
>
> He shouldn't have been …(eg driving so fast).

## Speaking

Below is a list of social and environmental problems experienced by many countries. **Tick those problems which are present in your country and then explain who you think is responsible for them.**

- Traffic congestion in large cities ☐
- Poor performance of national teams in international sporting events ☐
- Tax avoidance ☐
- Unemployment ☐
- Stress-related illnesses ☐
- Declining standards of education ☐
- Drug abuse ☐
- Other – _____ ☐

TEACHER'S NOTES **13A**

 **Trends**
Social trends

> **Theme:** Talking about social and economic trends.
>
> **Main language points:** Describing change (verbs of growth and decline + prepositions) and giving reasons for it.
>
> **Listening type:** A radio news report (dense and quite fast). Students check their predictions and record the numbers and statistics they hear.
>
> **Speaking type:** Students discuss social and economic trends in their countries.

Discussion

Ask the students to consider how affected they are by trends in the various areas listed and then to discuss the concept of fashion. If you like, you can teach (before or after the discussion) pertinent phrases such as: *fad, craze, trendy, fashion-conscious, to be in/out of fashion, to keep up with/up-to-date, to be influenced by*.

Vocabulary

Ask the students to read the words aloud and check their pronunciation. Then get them to complete the first exercise in pairs. Check the answers in open class. Pay particular attention to the difference between *rise* and *raise*, how *deteriorate* and *decline* are applied, the movable stress of *increase* and *decrease*, and the past forms of *fall* and *rise*.

**Possible answers**

1 *decrease/reduction/increase*
2 *fell/dropped/decreased/went down*
3 *increase/rise*
4 *deteriorated*
5 *doubled*
6 *increase*
7 *decline/fall/deterioration*
8 *raising*
9 *rising/going up/increasing*
10 *increase*

Ask students to study the prepositions *by, in, of, from, to* in the first vocabulary exercise and to comment on how they are used, eg *in* precedes the subject of the change as in *reduction in taxes*. Then ask them to do the next exercise. Check their answers in open class and then discuss the meaning of the highlighted adjectives and adverbs. They could try to illustrate these differences in the rate of change using a line graph.

**Answers**

1 *from* £30 000 *to* £40 000
2 *by* 1 per cent
3 *on* the increase/decline *in* air quality
4 *of* 15 per cent *in* the value
5 *Over* the next few years/rise *in* the number
6 improvement *in* the quality
7 levelled off *at* 2.5 per cent

Listening

Focus the students' attention on the ten statements and ask them to discuss in pairs how likely each one is to be true. Play the tape and ask them to mark each statement T (true) or F (false). Play the tape again and get them to note down the exact results of the survey.

# 13B Teacher's notes

 News report on social trends

**DF** = Denise Fletcher   **Newsreader** = male

**Newsreader:** … leaders will meet in Washington later today to discuss the growing economic rift between the two countries. At home a report on social and economic trends has just been published revealing that although we're working harder, we don't seem to be getting any better off – unless, that is, you are one of the richest 10%. Denise Fletcher has more details. So Denise, is it time to emigrate or not?

**DF:** Well, you might think so, going by these figures – about 12% more Britons are emigrating than four years ago. But it's still not a great number and it's actually outstripped by the number of people coming in.

**Newsreader:** Isn't the weather and the food keeping them at bay?

**DF:** Well, not really: the quality of food here does seem to be improving – last year there were considerably less complaints about the food served in public bars and restaurants than the previous year and we are eating healthier food as well, it seems.

**Newsreader:** For example?

**DF:** Such as … products which are high in cholesterol, like butter and full-fat milk – consumption of these has halved in the last ten years, while the great British favourite, the potato, is down 15%. The couch potato on the other hand is flourishing. Last year the average Briton watched 27 hours of television per week.

**Newsreader:** I wondered where my audience had gone.

**DF:** Leisure in general is a growth industry. There has been a steady increase in the amount of time and money spent on leisure and this is reflected in the number of holidays abroad that people now take: a quarter of the adult population can afford to take two holidays a year.

**Newsreader:** That sounds very encouraging, but has more leisure time and an improved diet made us any healthier?

**DF:** Well, yes, it has. Life expectancy has actually risen by 5% in the last 20 years to 73 for men and 78 for women. Smoking is down by about 10% on ten years ago, although interestingly the fastest growing group of smokers is teenage girls.

**Newsreader:** And what were the most striking statistics in the report?

**DF:** Perhaps the most dramatic changes have come in the make-up of the family, and especially the role of women. Many more women are now economically active and a good proportion of these are single mothers: in fact in the last ten years the number of single parent families has gone up by a staggering 25%.

**Newsreader:** And why are so many more women working? Is it out of necessity as you're suggesting or is it also a matter of choice?

**DF:** The study doesn't provide reasons, but there's no doubt that times have got harder for the vast majority of the population. The gap between rich and poor has never, in the last fifteen years, been so marked. The income of the poorest tenth has dropped by 17% whilst the richest tenth found themselves richer by 62% .

**Newsreader:** And on that cheerful note we must leave you. If you're now thinking of emigrating, you may pick up some useful hints in today's edition of the *Travel Show* at 10 am. For listeners in Wales there will be …

**Answers**

1 *True (12% more are emigrating, but even more are immigrating.)*
2 *True (There are fewer complaints about food served in public places.)*
3 *True (15% down)*
4 *True (27 hours)*
5 *False (a quarter of the adult population)*
6 *True (by 5%)*
7 *False (Many more are working.)*
8 *True (25% in the last ten years.)*
9 *True (17%)*
10 *True (62%)*

## Speaking

Draw the students' attention to the language box and go through it asking them to complete each phrase using education as an example, for example, There has been a steady increase in *the number of people going into higher education*.

Now ask the students to study the different areas of change and to select two or three that they know about to comment on. Give them a few minutes to prepare what they are going to say and then ask them to discuss their views in groups.

TASK SHEET **13A**

# 13 Trends

## Social trends

**Discussion**

To what extent are you affected by trends in the following?

clothes
diet
styles of music
physical exercise
interior design
language use
information technology

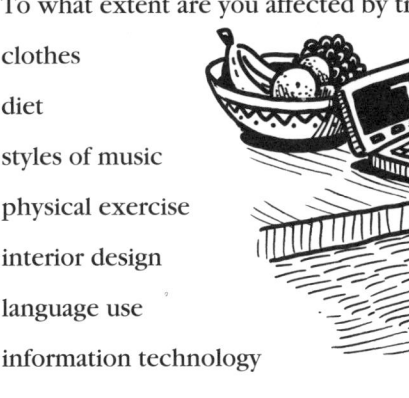

In what area do you follow developments most closely? Does the word 'fashion' have positive or negative connotations for you?

**Vocabulary**

**Use the words in the box to complete the sentences below, putting the verbs into the correct tense. Note that sometimes more than one answer is possible.**

| rise | fall | boom | increase |
| decrease | raise | drop | reduce |
| lower | deteriorate | improve | go down |
| decline | reduction | go up | double |

1 We welcome the recent _____ in taxes announced in the Chancellor's speech.

2 To the relief of the government, unemployment _____ last month by 90 000.

3 The _____ in drug-related crime is very disturbing.

4 Relations between the two countries have _____ since the refugee crisis started.

5 The number of divorces has nearly _____ from 10 000 to 19 000.

6 An _____ of 20% in the number of people claiming pensions over the last ten years has left governments wondering what they can do.

7 Most people admit that there has been a worrying _____ in broadcasting standards.

8 The government is thinking of _____ the school leaving age by one year to seventeen.

9 In spite of higher import duties, the demand for foreign luxury goods is still _____ after three years of recession.

10 Bike thefts are on the _____ despite police warnings.

PHOTOCOPIABLE

**13B** Task sheet

**Now complete the sentences below with the correct preposition and comment on the meaning of the adjectives and adverbs.**

1 The average salary has risen steadily _____ £30 000 _____ £40 000 as has people's standard of living.

2 Salaries have fallen slightly, _____ 1%.

3 Asthma cases are _____ the increase owing to a dramatic decline _____ air quality.

4 A sudden fall _____ 15% _____ the value of the dollar has shocked Wall Street.

5 _____ the next few years we can expect to see a significant rise _____ the number of people working from home.

6 There has been a marked improvement _____ the quality of food served in restaurants.

7 Inflation has levelled off _____ 2.5% following May's sharp fall.

## Listening

You are going to hear an extract from a news programme in which a recent survey on social trends in Britain is being discussed. **Before you listen, look at the sentences below and decide whether you think they are T (true) or F (false).**

1 More people are immigrating to Britain than four years ago. ☐

2 The quality of English food is improving. ☐

3 People are eating fewer potatoes than ten years ago. ☐

4 Last year the average Briton watched more than seventeen hours of TV per week. ☐

5 Most people go on holiday twice a year. ☐

6 Improvements in diet have helped to extend life expectancy. ☐

7 More women are opting to stay at home to look after their families rather than going out to work. ☐

8 The number of single mothers has risen sharply. ☐

9 The income of the poorest tenth of the population has fallen. ☐

10 The income of the richest tenth has risen sharply. ☐

TASK SHEET **13C**

🔊 Now listen and mark the sentences T (true) or F (false) again according to what the report says. Also, make a note of the exact figures or statistics to justify your answer.

Speaking

Choose two or three of the subjects below and, using the language box to help you, describe the trend in your country.

- ☆ Political views
- ☆ Modes of transport
- ☆ Industry
- ☆ Spending habits
- ☆ Eating habits
- ☆ Holidays
- ☆ How people spend their leisure time
- ☆ Attitudes to medicine and health
- ☆ Family life and the roles of men and women
- ☆ Crime
- ☆ Other - _____

---

**Up to now**

Over the last ten years/Recently …

There has been a steady increase in …

**Present**

It is becoming increasingly (difficult) to …

More and more people are …-ing …

There's a growing (realization that) …

There's a trend towards …

**Cause and effect**

This is due to/because of/a result of … (eg changes in attitude)

(eg Changes in attitude) have led to/meant that…

(eg Changes in attitude) had a lot something/nothing to do with …

---

PHOTOCOPIABLE

© David Briggs, Paul Dummett 1995. Published by Heinemann English Language Teaching. This sheet may be photocopied and used within the class.

# 14A Teacher's notes

# Trends
## A crisis meeting

> **Theme:** Describing market trends.
>
> **Main language points:** The language of meetings and debate.
>
> **Listening type:** A group discussion – business meeting (background noise and interruptions). Students complete a graph.
>
> **Speaking type:** Discussing options and deciding on the best course of action; language of meetings.

## Vocabulary

Give out the task sheet and focus the students' attention on the business vocabulary. Ask them to practise saying the words to each other in pairs and to mark where the stress falls in each word.

**Answers**

| | |
|---|---|
| 'turnover (= total annual sales) | a com'petitor |
| to ˌundercut (a competitor = to sell at a lower price) | ˌcompe'tition |
| | to with'draw (a product = not to sell anymore) |
| 'profit margin | to 'offset – ˌoff'set (losses = to balance against) |
| a (ˌretail) 'outlet (= a shop) | to out'sell |
| a sup'plier | an 'outlay ( = expenditure) |

Check the pronunciation and the meanings of the words with the whole class.

## Listening

Go through the background information about the company and ask the students what factors might affect the sales of poultry products. Then focus their attention on the graph and ask them to complete it as they listen. Tell them not to try to draw in the columns as they listen, but to do this once they have listened for and noted down the figures. Play the listening passage and ask them to check their answers in pairs.

 A board meeting

**Amanda, John** and **Bill**

**Amanda:** OK. To begin with, let me just say I'm sorry about bringing you in so early on a Monday morning, but I felt that a meeting was necessary. Yesterday the buyer for St Cotes Supermarkets rang me to say that they were thinking of withdrawing our fresh corn-fed chickens from the shelves. Yes, that's right … but it's not totally out of the blue. So I thought I'd get you here to give you an update on the situation and discuss what action we should take, because we must act quickly. Time isn't on our side. So, Bill's going to summarize the background … Bill …

**Bill:** Thanks, Amanda. I think before I talk about the most recent events, it'd be helpful to remind ourselves of what's been happening over the past year. For that reason I've prepared this graph which shows the development of sales of chickens since last August. As you can see, our problem began in the latter half of last year – and we put this down to the competition from the Dutch company, Van Lyken. Chicken was their loss leader in a range of meat products, and none of us really expected this to pose any problem in the long term. As you can see sales dropped to

£390 000 for October and November; December was even worse – but fortunately for us that was offset by sales of turkeys. But the major recovery that we all expected in the New Year never materialized – there was a slight rise in January of 5%. The problem was compounded when Van Lyken took the Safefare contract. It was then that we decided to launch the fresh corn-fed chickens – earlier than we had planned, but we had to take action quickly.

**John:** And it worked.

**Bill:** Yes, considering the minimal outlay on advertising; sales in the first month, February, reached £90 000. By April we'd really made a significant impact on the market and sales of fresh corn-fed were matching sales of regular frozen chicken and were set to start outselling them. But it was then that *Newsnight* broadcast their report on the salmonella cases in the Wickstead Old People's Home in Sheffield ... which blamed *our* fresh corn-fed chickens for the three deaths. As you can see on the graph, the sales plummeted to £40 000 in May and they haven't recovered, even though the link has still to be proved.

**John:** Hasn't the message got through to the public that it was the way it was cooked, not the chicken itself?

**Bill:** It seems not. The only consolation is that sales of frozen chicken are holding steady: if anything they're rising: rather ironically, in fact, as the danger from frozen chicken is no greater than from fresh corn-fed.

**Amanda:** Yes (sigh) that's the situation. Well, nothing much has changed except the urgency to do something about it. I need hardly say that losing the St Cotes order would be a devastating blow to us.

## Answers

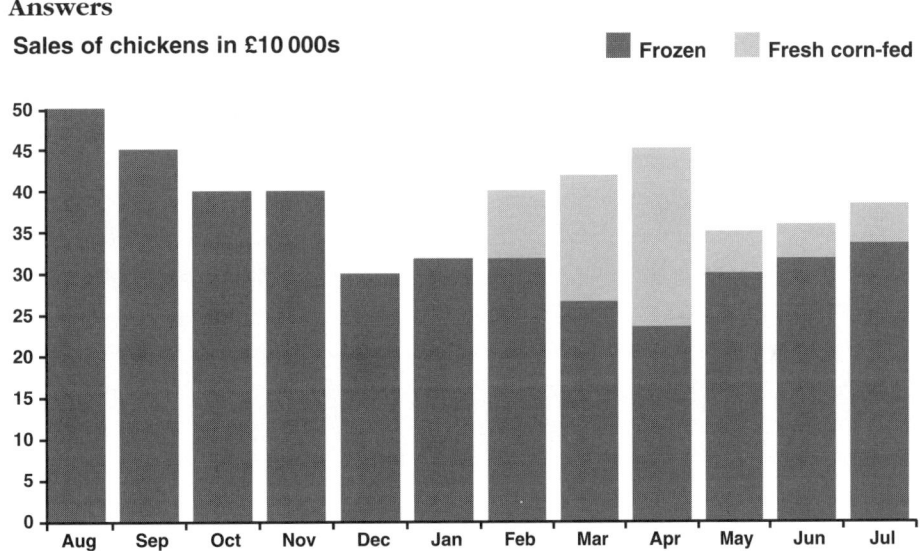

Sales of chickens in £10 000s — Frozen / Fresh corn-fed

Before playing the passage again, see if the students can answer any of the questions and then play it again to elicit the other answers.

## Answers

1 *The threat of losing the St Cotes contract.*
2 *Competition from the Dutch company Van Lyken.*
3 *Because of sales of Christmas turkeys.*
4 *They won a contract with the supermarket Safefare.*
5 *Because they had not invested much in advertising the new product.*
6 *The way it was prepared/cooked.*
7 *It has risen, even though the risks of salmonella poisoning are just as great from this as from fresh corn-fed chicken.*

# 14C Teacher's notes

## Speaking

In order to practise the phrases in the language box, write the following on the board:

*Aim of meeting: To decide which members of staff to lay off.*
*Background: Sales have fallen and there is not enough work.*
*Options:   To lay off more junior staff.*
             *To lay off most expensive staff.*
             *To lay off least flexible staff.*
*Recommendations: To create a points system using all these factors.*

Ask the students to work in small groups and to go through these points using the relevant phrases from the language box, eg *As you may know, sales have fallen and ...*; *I suggest that we lay off the most expensive staff ... ; I think it would be worth keeping the most flexible staff ...*

Before giving out the role cards, ask the students to work in pairs to make a list of the options available to Happy Valley Poulterers. Then put them into groups of four (three is also possible), preferably not students from the same pair. The reason for this activity is so that their contribution in the role-play is not determined only by what is on the role card.

Give them each a different role card and ask them to study it and prepare for the meeting. Give them three or four minutes to do this. Appoint someone to act as chairman or woman and then ask students to discuss the situation and decide on a course of action. If your students have some business background or, in your view, will be able to come up with strong arguments unaided, you can give them only the agenda and not the role cards.

Ask each group to present its decision and the reasons for it to the class.

TASK SHEET **14A**

# Trends

## A crisis meeting

**Vocabulary**

**Practise saying the words below to each other and mark where the stress falls.**

| turnover | to undercut | profit margin | a (retail) outlet |
| a supplier | a competitor | competition | to withdraw |
| to offset | to outsell | an outlay | |

**Listening**

Happy Valley Poulterers is a company which produces poultry products for the British domestic market. Its range of products includes chickens, both frozen (battery-farmed) and fresh (corn-fed), which it sells primarily through supermarkets.

You are going to hear three managers describing the events which have led to a crisis in the sales of these chickens. **Listen for the missing data in order to complete the graph below. Do not try to draw in the columns as you listen, but note down the figures and complete the graph afterwards.**

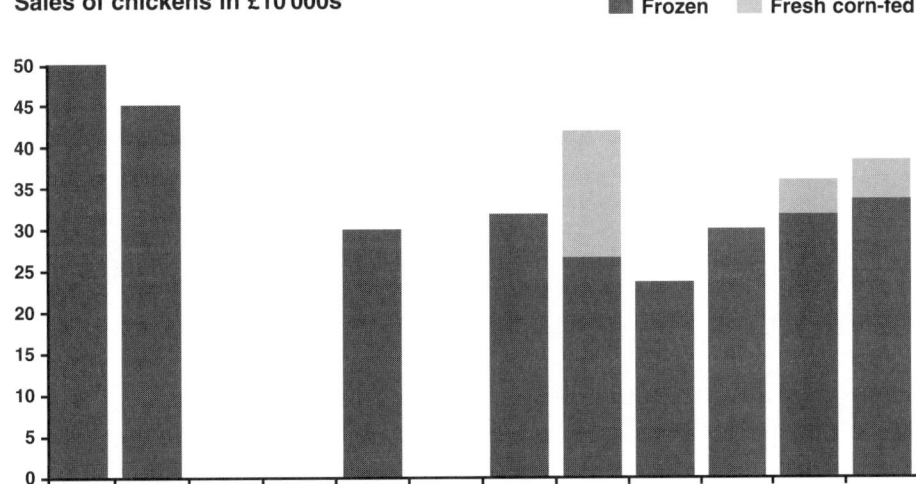

 Now listen again and answer these questions.

1 What event led to this emergency meeting being called?

2 What caused the initial decline in sales of frozen chicken?

3 Why wasn't December as bad a month as it might have been?

4 What did Happy Valley's competitors do in January?

5 Why were they surprised by the good performance in February?

6 To what does he attribute the incidence of salmonella poisoning at the old people's home?

7 What is ironic about the performance of frozen chicken in the last three months?

© David Briggs, Paul Dummett 1995. Published by Heinemann English Language Teaching. This sheet may be photocopied and used within the class.

## 14B Task sheet

**Speaking**

You are going to take part in a meeting to decide on the best course of action for the company to take now. There are many possibilities ranging from withdrawing the product at one extreme, to completely ignoring the bad publicity at the other. **Make a list of the possibilities.**

**Now study your role card and prepare for the meeting.**

### AGENDA

1 The product – Is there a problem?
2 The market – What is the demand?
3 The media – Is there anything that can be done?
4 Possible actions – Long term
　　　　　　　　　　 Short term

---

**Starting a meeting**

OK. Shall we begin?

Right. I think we ought to get started.

The aim of this meeting is to …

As you (may) know, …

**Making suggestions**

I suggest/recommend/propose　　　　　　　　　　doing …

　　　　　　　　　(that) we (should)　　do …

I think it would be worth …-ing …

It might be advisable/necessary to …

**Agreeing and disagreeing**

Yes, I'd go along with that.

To be honest/With respect, I don't think that's right.

**Concluding**

So, can we agree that …?

Let's summarize what we've agreed.

© David Briggs, Paul Dummett 1995. Published by Heinemann English Language Teaching. This sheet may be photocopied and used within the class.

Task sheet 14C

## The Technical Consultant

You want to face the problem and admit to your customers that changes need to be made. Your strategy is:

☆ to temporarily suspend the sales of fresh corn-fed chickens.

☆ to change the name fresh corn-fed to 'free range'.

☆ to emphasize this fact in advertising and on the packaging.

☆ to give clear warnings about the dangers of not defrosting or cooking chicken properly.

## The Marketing Manager

You think an aggressive marketing strategy is the only way to combat the adverse publicity that the company has received. Your strategy is:

☆ to suspend all advertising for one month.

☆ to push the products with a new advertising campaign.

☆ to persuade big customers that the salmonella poisoning could have happened with any brand of chicken.

## The Public Relations Officer

You are worried that changing the product will seem like an admission of guilt and will harm the company's image in the long-term. Your strategy is:

☆ to deny that the salmonella incident had anything to do with the type of chicken involved.

☆ to commission a medical report on the causes of salmonella, highlighting all possible sources of the disease.

☆ to open a research fund for investigation into the causes and treatment of salmonella.

## The Managing Director

You are broadly in favour of a wait-and-see policy. Your strategy is:

☆ to withdraw the fresh corn-fed chickens from the shops.

☆ to conduct market research after six months to see whether or not the public is still worried about the risks of salmonella.

☆ to relaunch fresh corn-fed chicken after eight or nine months if the results of the research are positive.

☆ to try to build up sales of frozen chicken in the meantime.

PHOTOCOPIABLE

© David Briggs, Paul Dummett 1995. Published by Heinemann English Language Teaching. This sheet may be photocopied and used within the class.

# 15A Teacher's notes

# Social English
## Anecdotes

> **Theme:** Recounting a story.
>
> **Main language points:** Narrative devices.
>
> **Listening type:** An anecdote about a chance meeting. (Fast idiomatic speech; Scottish accent.) Students answer detailed comprehension questions.
>
> **Speaking type:** Students tell an anecdote.

**Discussion**  Give the task sheets to the students and ask them to answer the questions, first in pairs and then with the whole class.

**Listening**  Focus the students' attention on the first three questions and then play the listening passage. Get the students to check their answers in pairs.

 The day I met Sean Connery

Taken from BBC Radio 4, 30 September 1994.

**SM** = Susie Maguire

**SM:** And there I was standing right next to Sean Connery. He was ginormous. I could've touched him. I could even have spent hours touching him if the lift had got stuck. But it didn't. I just had a few minutes to gaze at the middle bits of him out of the corner of my eye, and take in the aftershave and notice the freckles on the backs of his hands, and then the lift stopped. I stood aside and sort of waved my hand meaning 'You go first', but he did that thing with his eyebrows that makes his nostrils flare and said 'Ladies first,' and I swear to God I nearly melted into a wee heap. Anyway, I got my legs moving, left, right, left, right, out of the lift and then pretended to be really fascinated in this manky painting which had sort of twigs and stuff on it, not Joan Eardley, but some pathetic student rip-off merchant's idea of a winter landscape. I was keeping my ears open as they went past me down another blue corridor and through a door at the bottom. All I heard was the words 'tea' and 'make-up'. I started to think, 'What am I doing here, what do I want? If I do get to talk to him, what am I going to say?' and stuff like that. I didn't want to go in and ask for his autograph like some silly wee lassie. It had to be something else. Then I had a blinding revelation. Shortbread! He must really miss shortbread in Marbella. I went pelting down the stairs to the first floor canteen. I got a tray full of tea, coffee, real milk, sugar and a huge plate of tartan-wrapped individual bits of shortbread. I carried it very, very slowly to the lift and went back up to the fourth floor and down the corridor to Sean. I took a deep breath and knocked on the door. He said 'Come in' and I swear there was a wee lisp there, even on those two words. So in I went and he was sitting at a sort of Hollywood-style make-up table with millions of light bulbs around it and smart suit trousers and a white shirt, combing his moustache. Our eyes met through the mirror and I nearly died! He said 'Ah, tea'. 'Or coffee if you'd rather', I said. 'BBC coffee is always terrible', he said with his wee smile and I nodded like I knew what he meant. And I did. I poured him the tea, put the milk and sugar to hand, the teaspoon in the saucer, and pushed the plate of shortbread until it was practically under his chin. 'I bet you've not had this for a wee while', I said. 'Go on – put some in your pocket for later. I always get peckish when I'm trying to go to sleep and have to sneak a biscuit.' I could hardly look at him, like I didn't want to actually see him in case he disappeared. But he sort of laughed, and I did look, and he has these incredible eyes – dead crinkly and deep, and it's like taking some powerful illegal substance or something – I just felt a big WHOOSH – like, I've met Sean Connery and I can do anything. Incredible.

# Teacher's notes 15B

**Answers**
1 *Sean Connery – she was overcome and didn't say anything.*
2 *She brought tea, coffee and biscuits/shortbread to him in his dressing room.*
3 *He was polite and reasonably friendly.*

Play the passage again, this time asking the students to answer the second set of questions. Go through the answers first in pairs and then with the whole class.

**Answers**
1a *He was very large (ginormous) and had freckles on the backs of his hands.*
1b *He had crinkly eyes (with laughter lines).*
2 *She was overwhelmed and went weak (nearly melted into a wee heap).*
3 *A poorly painted (manky) winter landscape, copied (rip-off) from a more reputable artist.*
4 *She didn't want to appear childish (a silly wee lassie).*
5 *Because he lives in Marbella and shortbread is difficult to find outside the British Isles.*
6 *Tea, coffee, real milk, sugar and a huge plate of tartan wrapped individual bits of shortbread.*
7 *He was sitting at a dressing table combing his moustache.*
8 *He thinks that BBC coffee is terrible.*
9 *Because she always finds it useful to keep some aside in case she feels hungry in the night.*
10 *It was like taking some powerful drug.*

## Narrative devices

Ask the students what makes a good anecdote and what keeps the listener's attention. Focus their attention on the phrases from the listening passage and ask them to match each one to the correct type of speech. Go through the answers in open class.

**Answers**
There I was, standing … – *Participial clause*
In I went … – *Change in word order (for emphasis)*
… millions of light bulbs … – *Hyperbole (exaggeration)*
Anyway, … – *Returning to the story after a digression*
I nearly died. – *Hyperbole (exaggeration)*
He said, 'Ladies first'. – *Direct speech*
It was like taking an illegal substance. – *Simile*

NB *There I was* … is a common way of focusing the listener's attention on a key moment in the story and can be used to return to the point after a digression.
*In I went* … This type of inversion is most likely to be found in adverbial phrases of place.

Now ask the students to complete the five sentences with examples of the devices above. (If you like, you can then ask them to create their own sentences.)

## 15C Teacher's notes

**Suggested answers**
1 ... *a large Alsatian bearing its teeth.*
2 ... *a huge grizzly bear.*
3 ... *wanted the earth to open up and swallow her.*
4 ... *you couldn't lift your glass to your mouth.*
5 ... *that's right, the doctor. Well, he asked me to ...*

Speaking

Ask the students to prepare to tell a brief anecdote using one of the suggested topics. Encourage them to incorporate into their story at least two of the narrative devices they have practised.

# Social English

## Anecdotes

**Discussion**

Have you ever met anyone famous? Who would you like to meet and why?

If you were in a lift with someone famous, how would you strike up a conversation with them?

**Listening**

 You are going to hear an account of an encounter with a famous person. **Listen and answer the questions below.**

1 Who did the girl meet in the lift and what did she say to him?

2 How did she contrive to see him again?

3 What was his attitude to her?

 **Now listen again and answer the questions below.**

1 What physical features did she notice about him

   a) in the lift?

   b) in the make-up room?

2 How did she react when he spoke to her?

3 What was the painting like?

4 Why didn't she just ask him for his autograph?

5 Why must he miss shortbread?

6 What did she have on the tray?

7 What was he doing when she entered the room?

8 Why didn't he want coffee?

9 Why did she suggest he put a bit of shortbread in his pocket?

10 What did she compare the experience to?

## Narrative devices

The phrases from the tapescript below are examples of devices often used in the telling of anecdotes. **Match each one with the correct type of speech in the box.**

There I was, standing …   In I went …   … millions of light bulbs …

Anyway, …   I nearly died.   He said, 'Ladies first'.

It was like taking an illegal substance.

> Hyperbole (exaggeration)   Change in word order (for emphasis)
> Direct speech   Simile
> Returning to the story   Participial clause
> after a digression

**Now think of ways to complete the following sentences.**

1 Coming towards me, at an alarming speed, was _____.

2 At the entrance to the cave stood a _____.

3 The girl looked as if she _____.

4 The little room was so packed that _____.

5 Where was I? Ah, yes, _____.

## Speaking

**Choose one of the following topics and prepare to tell a brief story to your partner. The story can be true or false, but don't tell the others in the class – let them guess which it is.**

The time that you …

☆ met someone famous.

☆ met your partner for the first time.

☆ were terrified or afraid for your life.

☆ lost something really important.

☆ were given the credit for something you didn't do.

☆ were unjustly treated.

☆ committed a faux pas.

☆ Other – _____

TEACHER'S NOTES **16A**

# Social English
## Saying the right thing

> **Theme:** The English used in everyday social situations.
>
> **Main language points:** Short responses: accepting, apologizing, offering, speculating, thanking, etc.
>
> **Listening type:** A series of short statements or questions in a variety of everyday situations. Students are asked to make an immediate response.
>
> **Speaking type:** Short conversational exchanges using appropriate functional phrases.

Discussion

If you can, give an example from your own experience of being at a loss to know what to say in a particular social situation in an English-speaking country. Ask the students to work in pairs to do the same and to answer the other questions. Then ask students to work with someone with the same first language to make a list of five key phrases in that language for different situations. Go through these with the whole class asking them to translate their phrases into English and to comment on their application.

Vocabulary

Make copies of the task sheet with the cards on them for each pair of students. Cut up the statements or questions (marked **A**) and cut up the answers (marked **B**) and shuffle them, keeping the two sets of sentences separate. Give one complete set to each pair and ask them to match each sentence **A** with appropriate responses **B**. (Note: There are two or three responses which go with each **A** sentence.) Check the answers with the whole class.

**Answers**
- I can't seem to get this collar off the cat. It's rather fiddly.
- *I'll give you a hand, if you like/Here, let me have a go/Sorry. I'd help, but I'm allergic to them.*
- Thanks very much for filling in for me yesterday.
- *Not at all. Anytime/Don't mention it.*
- Well, I'm OK, but poor Kevin was laid off yesterday.
- *That's bad luck/Oh dear, I'm sorry to hear that.*
- Surely Sue's not going to get the assistant director's job, is she?
- *I doubt it very much/I shouldn't think so/With any luck she will.*
- I can get away early on Thursday. I'll pick you up at 4.30.
- *Sorry, I can't make it that day/That sounds fine/Actually, 5.00 would suit me better.*
- I'm afraid Mrs Davies can't be disturbed at the moment. Can I help you at all?
- *Actually, I really need to speak to her in person/That's alright. I'll call back later/Yes. Could you ask her to get back to me. It's about ...*
- Excuse me. You're standing on my toe.
- *I am sorry. I didn't realize/I do beg your pardon.*
- Do you fancy popping round for a drink later on?

## 16B Teacher's notes

   *– Yes, that'd be great/I'd love to, but I've got too much on. Sorry.*
- Would you like me to drop off the kids after school?
   *– Oh, that's very good of you. Thank you/Thanks. That would be a great help/It's alright. I wouldn't want to put you out.*
- Could I borrow your violin case? I'm going to a fancy dress ball tonight.
   *– Sure, go ahead/Well, actually I'd rather you didn't …*
- By the way, I'm going to be dropping in on Claudette when I'm in Paris.
   *– Are you? Give her my regards/Really? Say hello from me.*
- Thanks for the use of the car. I've filled it up, incidentally.
   *– Oh you needn't have/Oh that's very good of you. Thank you.*

Still working in pairs, ask the students to turn over all the **B** cards and to test each other by reading aloud the **A** sentences for the other student to respond to. Monitor them as they do this paying particular attention to their intonation.

### Listening and Speaking

Tell the students that they are going to hear ten situations to which they have to make quick and appropriate responses. Model the first one by playing the extract and answering it yourself. Play the other examples, pausing at the end of each situation and nominating a student at random to respond. Go through the listening twice if the students seem to find it difficult.

#### Ten everyday situations

1 A friend has been staying with you for one night while he's in town on business. As he leaves he says, 'Well, do drop in and see us the next time you're our way. And thanks again for putting me up at such short notice.'

2 You are about to leave your office for lunch. You telephone a client first and the receptionist says, 'I'm sorry Mr Allen's line is engaged at the moment. Would you like to hold?'

3 You're halfway through a meal and one of your guests has finished eating ahead of everyone else. She says, 'Do you mind if I smoke?'

4 You're trying to do some work at home when a particularly talkative neighbour comes to the door. He says, 'Hello. I've got a spare minute. Would you like to see those photos of Malta now?'

5 In the street you meet a colleague whom you thought was on holiday in Italy. She says, 'We were only there for three days, but we had to cut the holiday short because two of the kids picked up a nasty virus.'

6 You're waiting for some dinner guests whom you have invited from a sense of obligation rather than out of choice. Untypically, they are 30 minutes late. Your friend says, 'This is unusual. Do you think they've forgotten?'

7 A colleague is sitting in front of the computer looking exasperated. When you ask what the matter is, he says, 'I've been trying to load this programme for half an hour and it's driving me absolutely barmy.'

8 As you leave a bar you pick up what you think is your jacket. A man says, 'Hey, where do you think you're going with my jacket?'

9 You telephone a friend because you need to know if he is going to come to a party you are giving on Friday. A voice says, 'I know these machines are horrible, but take a deep breath, gather your thoughts and speak after the beep.'

10 You are trying to arrange a time to meet a friend to go to a show. You're not free until 6.30. Your friend says, 'Look, let's meet before the show and we could go for a drink first. Say, 6.15?'

**Suggested answers**
1 *Not at all. Anytime/Don't mention it.*
2 *That's alright. I'll call back later/Oh, could you ask him to get back to me.*
3 *Well, actually I'd rather you didn't/Sure. Go ahead*
4 *I'd love to, but I've got too much on.*
5 *Oh dear, I'm sorry to hear that. Are they OK now?*
6 *I shouldn't think so/With any luck they have.*
7 *Here, let me have a go.*
8 *I am sorry. I didn't realize.*
9 *Hello, it's me, Charlie. I was just wondering if you were going to be able to make it to the party on Friday.*
10 *Actually, 7.00 would suit be better.*

## Speaking

Make one copy of the task sheet and cut up the situations as indicated. Tell the students that they are going to act out two- to four-line dialogues for different situations. Read out the first situation and elicit the dialogue that it prompts (see answers below for a guideline). Ask them to work in pairs and to do the same for other situations. Give one situation to each pair. After two minutes tell each pair to pass their situation to the couple on their left. Discourage them from writing the dialogues down. When all the situations in circulation have been acted out by each pair, nominate pairs to present one of the dialogues to the rest of the class. Use your judgement in this to select those dialogues in which students used the language most naturally.

**Suggested answers**
A: *Is something the matter?*
B: *It's nothing. I've just got a lot on my mind with the Frankfurt Book Fair coming up.*
A: *Is there anything I can do to help?*
B: *I don't think so, thanks, but I appreciate the thought.*

A: *Look, I came across this old painting in the attic. I've no use for it. Would you like it?*
B: *Well, that's very kind of you, but it's not really my type of thing.*

A: *Well, thanks very much for having me. I hope it hasn't put you out too much.*
B: *Not at all, anytime.*
A: *And this is just a little something by way of a thank you.*
B: *Oh, you needn't have done that.*

A: *You're probably quite hungry by now. There's an Indian restaurant just round the corner. Shall we go?*
B: *That's very kind of you, but to be honest, I'm not very keen on hot food.*

A: *One fridge for 48 Beezely Street. Could you just sign here?*
B: *I'm sorry. There must have been some mistake. I haven't ordered a fridge.*
A: *You are Mr Hansard, aren't you?*
B: *No, I'm not. He lives two doors away.*

## 16D Teacher's notes

**A:** *Hello, I'm calling on behalf of Terry Merson. He's due to meet you for lunch tomorrow, but he's sorry he won't be able to make it. He's had to go to London at short notice.*
**B:** *That's funny, I was talking to his wife this morning and she didn't mention anything about London.*
OR *Oh, that's a shame. Well, thanks for calling anyway.*

**A:** *Sorry, I can't seem to locate the problem.*
**B:** *Oh well, thanks very much for trying. It was very kind of you.*
**A:** *Don't mention it. Only sorry I couldn't be of more help.*

**A:** *Here, let me give you a hand with those. Ooops! Oh my goodness, I am sorry.*
**B:** *Don't worry. They weren't good glasses.*
**A:** *Maybe not, but I'll replace them. Tell me where you got them from.*

**A:** *Do you like my new jacket?*
**B:** *Well, to be honest, it's a bit loud for my taste.*

**A:** *Hello. It's Claudia, isn't it? Do you remember me? We met at the Brighton conference, I think.*
**B:** *No, I don't think so. I think you're mistaking me for someone else.*
**A:** *Oh, I do beg your pardon. I could have sworn I recognized your face.*

**A:** *Can I give you a hand with that bag? You look as though you are struggling with it.*
**B:** *I may look decrepit, but I can still manage to carry a suitcase thank you.*
**A:** *Sorry, I didn't mean it to sound like that. I just wanted to help.*

**A:** *Didn't you find that your grandparents had so much more time for you as a child than your parents?*
**B:** *No, actually both my grandparents died before I was born.*
**A:** *Oh, I'm sorry ... my parents always seemed too busy to stop and enjoy us as children. It's different now, but ...*

TASK SHEET **16A**

# Social English

## Saying the right thing

Discussion

Have you ever been to an English-speaking country? Were there any situations in which you found yourself unable to think of an appropriate response quickly? Were there any situations in which you committed a faux pas (said the wrong thing)?

If you were to teach a foreigner five key phrases in your language that are unlikely to be in a standard phrase book, what would these be?

Vocabulary

You will be given some cards, some of which have statements or questions addressed to someone on them (marked **A**) and others which have short responses to these (marked **B**). **Find two or three responses for each statement or question.**

Listening and Speaking

You are going to hear ten situations in which you might find yourself. After each one you will be given a short time in which to respond. **Say what it seems natural to say. Use any of the phrases you have just seen that seem appropriate.**

Speaking

You will be given a card on which there is a description of an everyday situation. **Work in pairs to act out the situation. *Don't* write it down. When you have finished pass your card on to the next pair.**

## 16B Task sheet

**A**
I can't seem to get this collar off the cat. It's rather fiddly.

**A**
Thanks very much for filling in for me yesterday.

**A**
Well, I'm OK, but poor Kevin was laid off yesterday.

**A**
Surely Sue's not going to get the assistant director's job, is she?

**A**
I can get away early on Thursday. I'll pick you up at 4.30.

**A**
I'm afraid Mrs Davies can't be disturbed at the moment. Can I help you at all?

**A**
Excuse me. You're standing on my toe.

**A**
Do you fancy popping round for a drink later on?

**A**
Would you like me to drop off the kids after school?

**A**
Could I borrow your violin case? I'm going to a fancy dress ball tonight.

**A**
By the way, I'm going to be dropping in on Claudette when I'm in Paris.

**A**
Thanks for the use of the car. I've filled it up, incidentally.

**B**
I'll give you a hand, if you like.

**B**
Here, let me have a go.

**B**
Sorry. I'd help, but I'm allergic to them.

**B**
Not at all. Anytime.

**B**
Don't mention it.

**B**
That's bad luck.

**B**
Oh dear, I'm sorry to hear that.

**B**
I doubt it very much.

**B**
I shouldn't think so.

© David Briggs, Paul Dummett 1995. Published by Heinemann English Language Teaching. This sheet may be photocopied and used within the class.

TASK SHEET **16C**

---

**B**

With any luck she will.

---

**B**

Sorry, I can't make it that day.

---

**B**

Actually, 5.00 would suit me better.

---

**B**

That sounds fine.

---

**B**

Actually, I really need to speak to her in person.

---

**B**

That's alright. I'll call back later.

---

**B**

Yes. Could you ask her to get back to me? It's about …

---

**B**

I am sorry. I didn't realize.

---

**B**

I do beg your pardon.

---

**B**

Yes, that'd be great.

---

**B**

I'd love to, but I've got too much on. Sorry.

---

**B**

Are you? Give her my regards.

---

**B**

Really? Say hello from me.

---

**B**

Sure, go ahead.

---

**B**

Oh, that's very good of you. Thank you.

---

**B**

Well, actually I'd rather you didn't …

---

**B**

Thanks. That would be a great help.

---

**B**

It's alright. I wouldn't want to put you out.

---

**B**

Oh you needn't have.

## 16D Task sheet

---

Your boss has been pacing around the office all day looking worried.

**A** = Employee   **B** = Boss

---

A friend is sorting out her house and throwing out some things she doesn't want anymore. She offers you an old painting of a seascape, which you don't like at all.

**A** = Woman sorting out house   **B** = Friend

---

You have been in town on business and have been staying for one night with an old friend. As you are about to leave, you give her a bottle of wine.

**A** = Guest   **B** = Host

---

You are the guest of the Sales Manager in a company and are being shown around the factory. At the end of the tour he informs you that he has arranged for you to have lunch in an Indian restaurant, but you can't stand Indian food.

**A** = Sales Manager   **B** = Visitor

---

A delivery van arrives at your house and a man wheels a brand new fridge to the door, but you haven't ordered a fridge from anyone.

**A** = Delivery Man   **B** = Householder

---

You have to telephone someone you don't know to explain that your colleague cannot meet them for lunch tomorrow. Your colleague wanted to get out of the meeting and asked you to think up some likely excuse.

**A** = Caller   **B** = Person answering the call

---

Your car has broken down in the street. A passer-by stops and tries to find out what the problem is. He spends twenty minutes looking at the engine, but without success.

**A** = Passer-by   **B** = Motorist

---

You are helping a friend to clean up after a party and you see her struggling with a large tray of dirty glasses. You offer to help, but as you take the tray from her, you drop it.

**A** = Friend   **B** = Party Host

---

Your friend has just bought a new jacket (a hideous lime green checked sports jacket). He is obviously very pleased with it and asks you what you think of it.

**A** = Jacket owner   **B** = Friend

---

A complete stranger stops you in the street and asks you if you remember her from a conference in Brighton two years ago.

**A** = Stranger 1   **B** = Stranger 2

---

You offer to help someone to carry a bag that looks too heavy for him. He is angry at the suggestion that he is too old to manage.

**A** = Helpful stranger   **B** = Man with bag

---

Whilst talking to a friend about children you say that grandparents have more time to enjoy their company than parents do. Your friend says that she can't comment as she never knew her grandparents.

**A** = Friend 1   **B** = Friend 2

---

© David Briggs, Paul Dummett 1995. Published by Heinemann English Language Teaching. This sheet may be photocopied and used within the class.

TEACHER'S NOTES **17A**

# Humour
## Just a minute

> **Theme:** Humour
>
> **Main language points:** Verbs of joking (plus prepositions).
>
> **Listening type:** A radio panel game. Fast, humorous and with many cultural references. Students follow the rapid (and sometimes unexpected) developments in one round of the game.
>
> **Speaking type:** Students try to keep talking in English for a minute without hesitation.

Vocabulary and Discussion

Play the following joke to illustrate what a practical joke is. When you go into the classroom, tell a student (one of the more resilient ones!) that there is a message from the office to say that a man from the BBC World Service is waiting for them at reception and would like to interview them about being a successful language learner. The office said that he only wanted a few words and would not take up too much of their time. Excuse the student from class. When he/she returns, ask the class (and the victim!) if they find this kind of joke funny.

Give out the task sheets and ask them to work in pairs to complete each of the sentences by using one of the prepositions in the box. Check the answers with the whole class.

**Answers**
*to make fun of someone/something*
*to laugh at someone/something*
*to tell/make jokes about something*
*to put someone down*
*to send someone/something up*
*to play a trick on someone*
*to poke fun at someone/something*
*to have someone on*

Then focus their attention on the three discussion questions and ask them to work in groups of three to answer them. Ask members of each group to report back on what they have learnt. Note: Students may also find these words useful when describing types of comedy: *(political) satire, farce, stand-up comedy, situation comedy, comedy of manners, slapstick, impressionists, alternative comedy.*

Listening

Tell the students that they are going to hear an extract from a popular radio programme called *Just a minute*. Ask them to listen for an explanation of the rules of the game and then play the introduction.

# 17B Teacher's notes

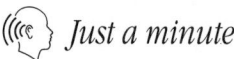 *Just a minute*

Taken from *Just a minute*, BBC Radio 4, 8 January 1994.

**NP** = Nicholas Parsons   **PM** = Paul Merton   **SF** = Stephen Fry

**NP:** (Clapping) Beside me sits Miriam Jones, who's going to keep the score and she's going to blow a whistle when the 60 seconds are up. And, as usual, I'm going to ask our four panellists to speak in turn, if they can, on the subject that I give them without hesitation, without repetition or deviating from the subject on the card.

Now ask the students to turn to their partner and explain the rules (*To speak for one minute on the subject given without hesitation, repetition or deviating from the subject*). Tell them that they are going to listen to one round of the game and that they should fill in the table by writing down what the subject is, what each interruption is for and whether the challenge is a correct one or not. Play the rest of the tape.

**NP:** … Paul, will you start the next round. The subject, Dimitri Shostakovitch (Laughter) … I don't know why they're laughing – he's probably one of your favourite composers. You have 60 seconds as usual.
**SF:** There's a gift, Paul, you now know he's a composer. (Laughter and clapping)
**NP:** 60 seconds, Paul, starting now …
**PM:** Dimitri Shostakovitch like his contemporary Igor Stravinsky was Russian by birth and his performance of his marvellous third symphony in 1921 stunned the Moscow crowd who had never heard such marvellous chromatic scales before explored in the world of classical music. Unfortunately by the time he was at the peak of these powers which would be round about the 1940s he brushed up against Joseph Stalin who at that time was dictator of all the Russias and this man said to Shostakovitch, 'I want you to write music' … (BUZZ)
**NP:** Stephen.
**SF:** I think it's the third music in fact. I let the second one go because I was so aghast.
**NP:** Yes, it was very impressive.
**PM:** I don't know why it's impressive that I should have heard of one of the leading classical composers of the twentieth century.
**NP:** What was impressive was the amount of information you packed into the 35 seconds that you spoke.
**PM:** It's all rubbish (Laughter), but it's the sort of stuff that would impress you. (Laughter and clapping) The audience have a general view that I'm fairly thick, but they are agreed that you're thicker than I am. (Laughter)
**NP:** Stephen, you had a correct challenge – a point – 25 seconds, Dimitri Shostakovitch, starting now …
**SF:** I think it was Sir Thomas Beauchamp, the well-known conductor (BUZZ)
**NP:** Paul …
**PM:** Deviation, it wasn't! (Laughter) It's mere rumour, it's a very popular fallacy, but he never did.
[**SF:** He was in a different country, wasn't he?]
**NP:** So your challenge presumably is deviation. We enjoyed the challenge, but it was incorrect. Stephen has another point. 24 seconds Dimitri Shostakovitch, Stephen, starting now …
**SF:** The aforementioned baton-swinger was asked if he'd ever conducted any Shostakovitch and he said 'No, but I once trod in some.' (Laughter) He was not a great admirer of that … (BUZZ)
**NP:** Paul, a challenge.
**PM:** This is deviation because he actually said it about Stockhausen.
**SF:** He's quite right, you know. (Clapping) It's amazing what they teach in metalwork, isn't it?
**PM:** Don't be fooled by the showbusiness veneer. Ha, ha, I never thought I'd say those words in anger.
**NP:** Sixteen seconds, Dimitri Shostakovitch, starting now …
**PM:** Well, he was this geezer who wrote nice tunes as far as I can work out and people used to hear them in the Russian salons and (BUZZ) …
**NP:** And Stephen, challenged.
**SF:** It's our second Russian.
**NP:** You did have a Russian before. Eleven seconds are left for Dimitri Shostakovitch, with you, Stephen Fry starting now …
**SF:** Dimitri Shostakovitch was born in the latter part of the last century to parents who … (WHISTLE)

# Teacher's notes 17C

Go through the answers first in pairs and then with the whole class.

**Answers**
Subject: *Dimitri Shostakovitch*
First interruption for: *Repetition of 'music'*
Correct or incorrect challenge: *Correct*
Second interruption for: *Deviation (although the challenge is premature – he had only just begun his sentence and there was not yet any claim to dispute.)*
Correct or incorrect challenge: *Incorrect*
Third interruption for: *Deviation (the anecdote was not about Shostakovitch, but Stockhausen)*
Correct or incorrect challenge: *Correct*
Fourth interruption for: *Repetition of 'Russian'*
Correct or incorrect challenge: *Correct*

Ask the students to read the questions before listening to the passage a second time. Play it and then go through the answers first in pairs and then with the whole class.

**Answers**
1 *He is assumed to be not very knowledgeable or well-educated.*
2 *He was amazed (aghast) at how knowledgeable Paul Merton was about this subject.*
3 *The amount of information about the composer that Paul Merton has at his fingertips.*
4 *They think of Paul Merton as stupid (fairly thick) and the game show host as more stupid still.*
5 *He means 'conductor' but cannot repeat the word without being penalised.*
6 *That he hadn't conducted Shostakovitch but he had once trod in some (implying that he and his compositions were dog excrement!).*
7 *'It's amazing what they teach in metalwork.' The implication is that Paul Merton is not well-educated and did not go to an academic school.*

## Speaking

Tell the students that they are now going to play the game themselves. Divide them into groups of four or five (four or five panellists and one rotating referee). They should play to the same rules but not include repetition as one of the infringements. Before the game let everyone choose and study a subject for five to ten minutes so that they are better prepared to speak. They can take notes at this stage but they cannot use them when they come to speak. Also, be lenient with hesitation!

# 17 Humour

## Just a minute

**Vocabulary and Discussion**

Complete the phrases below with a preposition from the box. Then discuss with your partner the meaning of each one, giving examples where you can.

> at   on   down   on   of   up   at   about

to make fun _____ someone/something

to laugh _____ someone/something

to tell/make jokes _____ something

to put someone _____

to send someone/something _____

to play a trick _____ someone

to poke fun _____ someone/something

to have someone _____

What television comedies are popular in your country?

Who or what are the jokes generally directed at?

Can you think of a comedian or a style of comedy that you don't like and say why not?

**Listening**

🔊 You are going to listen to a game called *Just a minute* taken from British radio. Listen to the introduction and then go through the rules of the game with your partner.

🔊 Now listen to one round of the game and complete the table below.

| | |
|---|---|
| Subject: | |
| First interruption for: | |
| Correct or incorrect challenge: | |
| Second interruption for: | |
| Correct or incorrect challenge: | |
| Third interruption for: | |
| Correct or incorrect challenge: | |
| Fourth interruption for: | |
| Correct or incorrect challenge: | |

© David Briggs, Paul Dummett 1995. Published by Heinemann English Language Teaching. This sheet may be photocopied and used within the class.

TASK SHEET **17B**

**Listen again and answer the questions below.**

1 Why does the audience laugh when the subject is given to Paul Merton?

2 Why did Stephen Fry not interrupt sooner for the repetition of 'music'?

3 What is it that impresses the game show host about Paul Merton's speech?

4 What does Paul Merton say the audience's view of the game show host and him is?

5 Why does Stephen Fry refer to Shostakovitch as the 'aforementioned baton swinger'?

6 What is Thomas Beauchamp reputed to have said about conducting Shostakovitch and what does this imply?

7 Complete the sentence 'It's amazing what _____.' What is the implication here?

Speaking

You are now going to play the same game. **Study the subjects below for five to ten minutes and prepare to speak about them.**

| Red | Space | Travel | Feet |
| Rice | Snow | China | Dreams |
| Elvis Presley | Dancing | Cowboys | Dogs |

© David Briggs, Paul Dummett 1995. Published by Heinemann English Language Teaching. This sheet may be photocopied and used within the class.

PHOTOCOPIABLE

# 18A Teacher's notes

# Humour
## Telling a joke

> **Theme:** Jokes.
>
> **Main language points:** Types of joke.
>
> **Listening type:** A series of jokes (variety of accents); a jigsaw listening in which students listen so as to be able to retell a joke verbatim.
>
> **Speaking type:** Retelling a joke; making a caption for a cartoon.

### Vocabulary and Discussion

Focus the students' attention on the types of joke and ask them to find the correct definition for each type. Go through the answers with the whole class.

**Answers**

a put-down – *a joke that makes another person appear small*
a pun – *a joke based on a word that has two meanings* [humorous use of words which sound the same or of two meanings of the same word]
offbeat humour – *an unusual or not obviously funny joke*
an epigram – *a witty and stylistically pleasing comment* [a short poem or saying expressing an idea in a clever & amusing way]
black humour – *a joke about a subject which is normally sad (eg death)*
a stock joke – *a joke using a commonly joked about subject (eg regional characteristics such as stupidity, stinginess, mother-in-law, police)*

Ask the students to work in pairs and tell each other a traditional joke from their country or region. Then ask each student to report back on what type of joke they heard.

### Listening and Speaking

Tell the students that they are going to hear seven jokes on the tape and that they must say which category of joke each one belongs to. Play the jokes, pausing after each one to allow students time to note down their answer. [unusual / unconventional]

### Types of joke

1 Why was ten frightened? – Because seven ate nine.

2 I always know when it's the mother-in-law at the door because as soon as they hear her knock all the mice start throwing themselves into the traps.

3 What's blue and white and sits in a tree? – A fridge wearing a denim jacket.

4 There once was an eccentric old boffin, [technician or scientist) slang]
  Who remarked in a fine fit of coughing:
  'It isn't the cough
  That carries you off,
  But the coffin they carry you off in.'

5 A cynic is a man who knows the price of everything and the value of nothing.

6 It's not the men in my life that count, it's the life in my men.

7 **Lady:** If you were *my* husband, I would put poison in your tea.
  **Man:** If you were my wife, madam, I would drink it.

# Teacher's notes 18B

Go through the answers first in pairs and then with the whole class.

**Answers**

1 *a pun*
2 *a stock joke*
3 *offbeat humour*
4 *black humour (not very black)*
5 *an epigram*
6 *an epigram*
7 *a put-down*

This next activity is a jigsaw listening. Divide the students into two groups A and B. Send group A into one room with a tape recorder and group B into a separate room. Ask them to listen to the joke and to practise retelling it to each other. When they feel confident that they can do this, the two groups should join up. Pair students from group A with students from group B and ask them to tell their jokes to each other.

 **JIGSAW LISTENING A**

There was this man sitting by his front window on Christmas Day. He looks out and he sees this snail coming up the front path. And he thinks, 'Oh no, not a snail leaving its trail of slime all up my path.' Anyway, the snail knocks on the door and the man goes and answers it. The snail looks up at him. 'Happy Christmas', it says. The man looks down at the snail and then kicks it as far as he can down the path.
A few months later, it's Easter Day. The man hears a tap at the door. He looks out of the window and says, 'Oh no, not that snail again' and he goes to the door. He opens the door and the snail looks up at him and says, 'What did you do that for?'

 **JIGSAW LISTENING B**

This bloke goes over to his mother-in-law's for dinner one Sunday. They sit down and have their Sunday dinner and after half an hour his mother-in-law says, 'Well, haven't you noticed anything different about me?' 'Oh, God', he thinks to himself, 'What is it?'
'Mmmm, you've had your hair done', he says.
'No, I haven't', she says.
'Umm, you're wearing a new dress?'
'No, I've had this one for years.'
'I've got it, you've lost weight?'
'No.'
'Er … You've changed the curtains?'
'No'
'OK, I give in. What is it?'
'I'm wearing a gas mask.'

## Speaking

Focus the students' attention on the two cartoons with captions and ask them to read them. Explain that they are going to enter a caption competition. Ask the students to work in pairs to write captions for as many of the four other cartoons as they can. When they are ready collect the cartoons, number each one and display them on a board or on the classroom wall. Invite the students to look at them all. (If you like, you can ask them to nominate the best caption for each cartoon by writing their choices on a piece of paper and submitting it to you.)

# 18 Humour

## Telling a joke

**Vocabulary and Discussion**

Match the types of joke on the left with the definitions on the right.

| | |
|---|---|
| a put-down | a joke based on a word that has two meanings |
| a pun | a joke about a subject which is normally sad (e.g. death) |
| offbeat humour | a joke using a commonly joked about subject (eg regional characteristics such as stupidity, stinginess, mother-in-law, police) |
| an epigram | an unusual or not obviously funny joke |
| black humour | a joke that makes another person appear small |
| a stock joke | a witty and stylistically pleasing comment |

Tell each other a traditional joke from your country or region. What type of joke did you hear?

**Listening and Speaking**

You are going to hear seven jokes. **Listen and decide which of the categories above they fall into.**

Now listen separately to another joke and then rehearse telling it. When you are ready, go back to your partner and exchange jokes.

**Speaking**

Look at the two examples of cartoons with captions and then work in pairs to write captions for as many of the other cartoons as you can.

"I'll have the steak"

# 19A Teacher's notes

# The media
# Newspapers

> **Theme:** Newspapers and how they cover the news.
>
> **Main language points:** Vocabulary to describe news coverage.
>
> **Listening type:** A monologue: a critique of the role of newspaper journalism. Students listen to pick out the main arguments in his thesis.
>
> **Speaking type:** Students conduct a survey of newspaper reading habits.

### Vocabulary

Ask the students to name as many British newspapers as they can. What do they know about them? Now focus their attention on the sentences and ask them to complete them. Get them to compare their answers with another student.

**Answers:**
*exclusive, circulation, tabloid, broadsheet, biased, coverage*

Ask the students what the characteristics of good journalism and bad journalism are (verbs like *report, sensationalize, exaggerate, entertain, inform,* etc should come up). Now ask them to work in pairs to match the verbs on the left with the nouns on the right. Note: There is sometimes more than one possibility.

**Answers**
*to report the facts* (or *the truth*) *to trivialize the issue*
*to distort the truth* (or *the facts*) *to expose a scandal* (or *the truth*)
*to mislead the public*

### Listening

Focus the students' attention on the headlines and ask them to think about what the missing words might be. Tell them that they must complete the headlines and also write the source of each. Play the listening passage.

 Newspapers

**AR** = Andrea Randall

**AR:** Journalists still like to think that they are writing the first draft of history and there is a tendency for them, when reporting important events to exaggerate their significance. One can of course sympathize with them for showing unbounded optimism when the event heralds an end to war or bloodshed as in the case of this week's news of the Israeli-PLO accord. ISRAELI PLO AGREEMENT ENDS 45 YEARS OF CONFLICT ran the *Times* headline. But is the paper really justified in making such claims, appealing as they may be? Most of the press in fact carried the same message, that mutual recognition by Israel and the PLO was historic in any number of ways. Peace had at last come to the Middle East, the chance of another world war now looked unlikely. The *Guardian* reported MIDDLE EAST ENTERS NEW ERA WITH HISTORIC ACCORD and the *Independent* spoke of ISRAEL'S RETURN TO THE LAND OF MILK AND HONEY. Is this really the case? In their eagerness to be the chroniclers of history, are even respected journalists in danger of sensationalizing the issues, ... of reporting events without due circumspection? Historians report

# Teacher's notes 19B

dramatic events; but they don't dramatize events in order to create history.
Overstated though the importance of the event may have been, the most important thing happening anywhere in the world yesterday was the Israeli-PLO agreement. Unless that is you happen to be a reader of, say, the *Daily Star*. MY DAD - THE SEX-MAD RAT was what that paper believed to be the most important story of the day. The PLO agreement made 90 words on page four. In the *Daily Mirror* it was MY TRAGIC WIFE FELT WORTHLESS by Georgie Fame. With the boring Middle East story getting a third of an inside page next to the weather. I have, before now, asked tabloid editors about their apparently perverse sense of news values which will put some Hollywood scandal on the front page and relegate a real news story to a three-inch box somewhere. They always have the same two defences - the first is that their readers are genuinely more interested in scandal than they are in politics, which might well be the case. And the second is that most of their readers get that sort of news from the broadcast media.

Students check their answers in pairs before going through them in class.

**Answers**

45 - The Times
ERA/ACCORD - The Guardian
MILK/HONEY - The Independent
DAD/RAT - The Daily Star
WORTHLESS - The Daily Mirror

Then ask the students to answer the two questions.

**Answers**

1 *broadsheet; tabloid*
2 *The broadsheets tend to exaggerate its significance; the tabloids disregard its significance.*

Now focus their attention on the next three questions and play the passage again. Students compare their answers in pairs.

**Answers**

3 *He welcomes it, but he is not convinced that it will last.*
4 *Journalists tend to dramatize the events they report; historians simply report dramatic events.*
5 *They say that people a) prefer scandal b) get political news from TV and radio.*

## Speaking

Give one copy of the questionnaire to each student and ask them to answer it first for themselves, writing their answers in the first column. When they have finished, ask them to mingle and interview two other people in the class. When they have filled in their questionnaires, put them in groups of six to collate their information and decide on the reading habits of the class. A spokesperson from each group then reports back and from this information the class should decide on the profile of a newspaper which would appeal to the majority of the class.

# 19 The media

## Newspapers

**Vocabulary**

Complete the sentences below with the correct word (the first letter has been given for you).

A story which no other paper has is called an e_____.

The Sun newspaper has a daily c_____ of 4 million.

There are two sizes of newspaper, t_____ and b_____. (In Britain the latter is usually associated with the more serious journalism.)

If a paper supports a particular political party, it is said to be b_____ in favour of that party.

Most people who buy the *Financial Times* do so because it has good c_____ of business news.

Now match the verbs on the left with a noun on the right.

| | |
|---|---|
| to report | the truth |
| to distort | a scandal |
| to mislead | the facts |
| to trivialize | the issue |
| to expose | the public |

**Listening**

You are going to hear a journalist reviewing the previous day's newspapers. As you listen, complete the headlines below and make a note of the name of the paper they came from.

**ISRAELI – PLO AGREEMENT ENDS _____ YEARS OF CONFLICT**
The _____

**MIDDLE EAST ENTERS NEW _____ WITH HISTORIC _____**
The _____

**ISRAEL'S RETURN TO THE LAND OF _____ AND _____**
The _____

**MY _____ – THE SEX MAD _____**
The _____

**MY TRAGIC WIFE FELT _____**
The _____

**Now answer these questions.**

1 What type of papers are the first three? The second two?

2 What is the speaker's criticism of each side of the press's treatment of the Israeli–PLO story?

 **Listen to the review again and answer the questions below.**

3 How does the speaker himself feel about the PLO agreement?

4 In what ways are journalists unlike historians?

5 How do tabloid editors defend their choice of front-page stories?

## Speaking

You are going to conduct a survey on the press in one or more countries. **Talk to at least two people. Look at the questions in the table below and add any extra information you find out.**

| Questions | Name | Name | Name |
|---|---|---|---|
| Which paper do you usually read? | | | |
| What type of news does it cover mainly? | | | |
| What is its political bias? | | | |
| Can you give the profile of a typical reader? (sex, age, occupation, etc) | | | |
| What is it that appeals to you about it? (unbiased coverage, investigative journalism, etc) | | | |
| What page do you turn to first? | | | |
| In what ways do you think it could be improved? | | | |

# 20A Teacher's notes

# 20 The media

## Radio news

> **Theme:** Radio news.
>
> **Main language points:** Idioms; passive reporting verbs.
>
> **Listening type:** A five-minute news programme. Students predict the content of the programme from the headlines. Listening and note-taking.
>
> **Speaking type:** Producing a radio news programme.

### Listening

Ask the class from which medium they prefer to get the news and why. Then write up the following headline on the board LEADING POLITICIAN DENIES INVOLVEMENT IN BLACKMAIL SCANDAL and elicit questions about the story (eg *Who is the leading politician? Who is being blackmailed? Why? What repercussions will it have for him and his party?*).

Now tell the students that they are going to think of similar questions about four radio news stories. Play the headlines to them and ask them to work in pairs to write their questions. When they are ready, ask them to read out their questions. Write some of the questions on the board (about four per story). Play the news passage and ask them to answer the questions and take notes on any other stories that feature. Check the answers with the whole class.

 Radio news

**JS** = Julian Smith   **PK** = Paul Knowles   **CD** = Corinne Dougal   **Newsreader** = female

[Pip - pip - pip - pip - peep.]
**Newsreader:** It's 8 o'clock on Wednesday 16th December. The headlines: Demonstrations by prisoners at Newgate Prison have intensified with a series of clashes between guards and inmates overnight. The Prime Minister has responded to his critics by highlighting the government's achievements over the past year. Controversy has arisen over the publication of last week's lottery winner. And a carpet bought in a junk shop in Croydon has fetched a record sum at auction.
The demonstrations by inmates at Newgate Prison over the suspension of prison visits intensified today with a series of clashes between guards and inmates. Early reports suggest that several people have been seriously injured and that possibly one inmate has died. Here's our home affairs correspondent, Julian Smith.
**JS:** The full extent of the cost of this protest, both in human and material terms, will not be known until the prison authorities resume control, but undoubtedly it will be heavy. So far two prison security officers have been taken to hospital and several others have sustained injuries. The protesters have now occupied the roof of E wing, reserved for serious offenders and, as I speak, are hurling tiles down into the yard below. So far the warden, Kenneth Bond, a well-known hard-liner, has rejected calls for mediation, insisting that to negotiate would be to play into the rioters' hands. Visits to the prison were suspended after an axe and a three-foot crowbar were found in a prisoner's cell last weekend.
**Newsreader:** The trial of Charlotte Hannah accused of murdering a man she thought to be a mugger, began in Northampton today. A large crowd of supporters gathered outside the court and cheered Ms Hannah on her arrival. The trial is expected to last a week.

# Teacher's notes 20B

In order to stem the flow of personal criticism levelled at him during the last month, the Prime Minister has insisted that despite the divisions within his party, it is ending the year in credit. Just days after the crushing defeat in the by-election, he says that although this year has been tough, he is proud of the party's achievements. Here's our political correspondent, Paul Knowles.

**PK:** It's an upbeat message from the PM showing that he's not prepared to be blown off course by the party's internal troubles. Writing in the *Sunday News*, he cites the 'good' news stories – rising exports, falling unemployment, low inflation, improved public services and reduced crime – as evidence that his government is steering the country towards greater prosperity. He appears to make light of the party's divisions over Europe, saying the argument tends to focus on extremist views, which are not representative of the mainstream of party opinion. 'My vision is of a Britain punching its weight in a Europe that works for the advantage of this wonderful country.'

**Newsreader:** A newspaper has revealed the name of last week's multi-million pound lottery winner. The decision by the *Sunday News* has been condemned by several MPs. More details from our media correspondent, Corinne Dougal.

**CD:** Despite last week's High Court decision freeing them to reveal the winner's name, the *Sunday News* has devoted the whole of its front page to pictures of the man and his wife and details of their personal life. The paper's editor, Peter Rogan, said it was not an invasion of privacy and had been deemed entirely lawful. He also maintained that publicity ensured that winners were genuine and reassured lottery players that there was no jiggery-pokery. But the Conservative MP, Roger Nail, said newspapers stank of hypocrisy on this issue and that the winner didn't deserve to be hounded by the press in this way.

**Newsreader:** In Derbyshire an anti-motorway campaigner has been arrested for endangering the lives of drivers on the M68. Mr Joseph Alexander made various attempts to disrupt the traffic on the motorway in order to draw attention to his campaign, including parking a caravan across the fast lane of the northbound carriageway. He has been remanded in custody and will appear in court tomorrow morning.

Allegations of payments to local politicians by three leading construction companies are being investigated by the serious fraud squad in London. According to a councillor in Dudley, an area set aside for the site of a new community centre for local residents has now been earmarked for the development of private luxury flats.

And finally, a carpet bought in a junk shop in Croydon for £30 was auctioned yesterday at Sotheby's for £810 000. The carpet, originally bought by Mr Samuel Jakes, a joiner from Lincoln, turned out to be a seventeenth-century Mogul floor-covering depicting hunting scenes, of which very few survive in good condition.

Now ask the students to look at the nine phrases and to decide in pairs what each refers to and means.

**Answers**

1 ... *refers to the prison warden who has a reputation for being strict with offenders.*
2 ... *means acting in a way which gives your opponent (here the rioters) an advantage.*
3 ... *means here to limit the constant criticism directed at the Prime Minister.*
4 ... *refers to the Prime Minister not wanting to abandon his political programme (a nautical metaphor).*
5 ... *the divisions are differences of opinion within the government which the Prime Minister wants to portray as being not too serious.*
6 ... *(a contrived boxing metaphor) refers to Britain surviving in the political arena with other strong European powers.*
7 ... *means here that in the lottery there was no deception on the part of the lottery organizers.*
8 ... *refers to the lottery winner's privacy not being respected by journalists who follow him or her like a pack of dogs.*
9 ... *refers to an area of land which has been designated for development of a new community centre.*

## 20C Teacher's notes

### Speaking

Tell the students that they are going to produce a four-minute radio news programme for a national radio station. Put them in teams of four or six and focus their attention on the instructions and flow chart on the task sheet. Go through the instructions, dealing with any queries as they arise.

Before handing out the sets of twelve stories to each group (cut up), make sure students understand that they must all participate in the writing of the first two or three stories. Thereafter they should divide themselves into reporters, editors and a newsreader and follow the steps on the flow chart.

When the students are ready to produce their programme either provide them with tape-recording facilities and send them to another room to record their programme OR ask them to perform 'live' in front of the rest of the class.

TASK SHEET **20A**

# The media

## Radio news

Listening

🎧 You are going to listen to a news bulletin. **Listen first to the headlines and then in pairs think of two or more questions about each story that you would like to be answered by the fuller version that you will then hear.**

**Now listen to the whole news and find answers to your questions. Make notes on any other stories.**

To what do the following phrases refer and what do they mean?

1 'a well-known hard-liner'

2 'play into their hands'

3 'stem the flow of criticism'

4 'he's not prepared to be blown off course'

5 'to make light of the divisions'

6 'punching its weight'

7 'there was no jiggery-pokery'

8 'hounded by the press'

9 'an area has been earmarked …'

Speaking

Acting as a news team, you are going to produce a four-minute radio news programme for a national radio station.

☆ Work in teams of four or six. Look at the stories and together choose the ones you think are worth including.

☆ In pairs write a first draft of two or three stories using the language box to help you.

☆ Now divide yourselves into a *newsreader*, *editor(s)* and *reporters*.

☆ The *editor(s)* should check the stories for mistakes; the *newsreader* will then practise reading them aloud. The *reporters* should gather and write more stories.

☆ Continue to gather and write (*reporters*), edit and correct (*editors*) and practise reading (*newsreader*) other stories until you have enough material for four minutes air-time.

☆ Finally choose three or four stories and include interviews in them. Plan these interviews: they can be rehearsed, but not written. Make sure that in the final programme everyone has a chance to speak (by using 'correspondents' or 'interviewees').

© David Briggs, Paul Dummett 1995. Published by Heinemann English Language Teaching. This sheet may be photocopied and used within the class.

PHOTOCOPIABLE

## 20B Task sheet

```
News team choose stories to include.
        ↓
Reporters prepare stories.
        ↓
Editors check them.
        ↓
Newsreader rehearses the presentation of the stories
(Interviews rehearsed at end).
        ↓
Finished news programme is presented.
```

### Reporting

It is widely believed that …

It has been alleged/claimed that …

He is understood/thought/believed/known to have (done) …

She is considered/reputed/rumoured to be (doing) …

He admitted to/denied (doing/having done) …

They have threatened to… (do) …, if …

The government has been accused of (doing) …

The government recommended/suggested that he (do/should do) …

People have been encouraged/urged to (do) …

### Newspeak

Our correspondent in … has more details.

Now over to our correspondent in …

Early reports suggest that …

# Heinemann Questionnaire

At Heinemann ELT we are committed to continuing research into materials development. We would be very interested to hear your feedback about this resource book. Please photocopy this form and send it to your local Heinemann office or to the address at the bottom of the form. Thank you for your help.

Name: ..................................................................

Name of school: ...................................................

Address of school: ...............................................

Average age of students: ....................................

Size of class: .......................................................

Frequency and length of lesson: .........................

Course materials currently used with class:

..............................................................................

..............................................................................

Supplementary materials currently used with class:

..............................................................................

..............................................................................

Please tell us if you have enjoyed using this photocopiable teacher's resource book. If not, please tell us why not; if you have, please tell us why.

..................................................................................................................................................................
..................................................................................................................................................................
..................................................................................................................................................................

What features do you like most about this resource book? What do you like least?

..................................................................................................................................................................
..................................................................................................................................................................
..................................................................................................................................................................

Do you have any suggestions for improvements?

..................................................................................................................................................................
..................................................................................................................................................................
..................................................................................................................................................................

What other kinds of materials would you like to see in a photocopiable format?

..................................................................................................................................................................
..................................................................................................................................................................
..................................................................................................................................................................

Please check the boxes below if you would like information about new materials or would like to help us in materials development.

I would like to receive information about materials for ...

- ❑ children  ❑ adults
- ❑ exams  ❑ readers
- ❑ secondary school students
- ❑ university students
- ❑ business English
- ❑ supplementary materials

Would you be willing to help us develop new materials to suit your needs? Yes, I would like to ...

- ❑ pilot materials in my classroom.
- ❑ answer questionnaires.
- ❑ discuss my needs with a Heinemann Representative.

Please return this form to:
Editor, Heinemann Teacher Resources, Heinemann ELT, Halley Court, Jordan Hill, Oxford OX2 8EJ, UK

If you would prefer to fax the form, please send to + 44 1865 314193.

© Heinemann Publishers (Oxford) Ltd. 1995